© THE BAKER & TAYLOR CO.

KOURION

KOURION

THE SEARCH
FOR A LOST
ROMAN CITY

David Soren and Jamie James

ANCHOR PRESS
Doubleday
NEW YORK LONDON TORONTO SYDNEY

An Anchor Press book
Published by Bantam Doubleday Dell Publishing Group, Inc.,
666 Fifth Avenue, New York, New York 10103

Anchor Press and the portrayal of an anchor are trademarks of Doubleday, a division
of Bantam Doubleday Dell Publishing Group, Inc.

Library of Congress Cataloging-in-Publication Data
Soren, David.
Kourion: the search for a lost Roman city/by David Soren
and Jamie James.
p. cm.
Bibliography: p.
1. Kourion (Ancient city). 2. Cyprus—Antiquities, Roman.
3. Romans—Cyprus—Kourion (Ancient city) 4. Earthquakes—Cyprus—
Kourion (Ancient city) 5. Excavations (Archaeology)—Cyprus—
Kourion (Ancient city)
I. James, Jamie. II. Title.
DS54.95.K68S67 1988   87-35206
939'.37—dc19
ISBN 0-385-24141-0

BG

CONTENTS

v

CONTENTS

CONTENTS

ACKNOWLEDGMENTS

AFTER THE EXPERIENCE of writing our first trade book, the authors take a fresh and appreciative view of these pages. Simply put, the story recorded herein could never have happened without the talents of the many people who worked at the Kourion excavation and of other scholars farther afield. We wish to express our gratitude to those who have made this book possible.

Sponsors of the excavations at Kourion have included the National Geographic Society (1984–87), the University of Missouri and the Walters Art Gallery (1978–81), the University of Arizona (1982 to the present), Dartmouth College (1978–80), the National Endowment for the Humanities (1979 and 1985), the University of Maryland—Baltimore County (1978–80), Johns Hopkins University (1981), and the Institute for Laboratory Sci-

ix

ence in Ventura, California (1984). Patrons include Giraud Foster and Richard Royall (in honor of his late brother, a Dartmouth alumnus). The project has also been generously supported by Fine Arts for Fine Causes, the Hellenic Cultural Foundation, Claire and Nathan Kolins, Vivienne Oxman, and Nancy O'Neill.

David Soren particularly wishes to express his thanks to Vassos Karageorghis, director of antiquities of Cyprus, for permission to dig at Kourion and for his continuing support of the excavation; and to Noelle Soren, his wife, who first suggested excavating at Cyprus. Together with Lawrence Stager, Jane Waldbaum, Anita Walker, and Ellen Herscher, she helped in the original effort to obtain permission for the project. Many of the photographs in this book are Noelle's work.

Particular thanks for financial aid must be given to the University of Missouri Alumni Development Fund and the Research Council, as well as to the Missouri Arts Council and the Archaeological Institute of America. The following scholars and their institutions have also contributed to the success of the Kourion dig: Warrant Officer Harry Heywood of the British forces on Cyprus and his wife, Audrey; Stuart Swiny, director of the Cyprus American Research Institute, and Helena Wylde Swiny, whose *Archaeological Guide to the Ancient Kourion Area* was a useful source, consulted often in the preparation of this text; Richard Jensen, classics professor at the University of Arizona; Roger Edwards of the University of Pennsylvania Museum; and Diana Buitron, codirector of the dig at the sanctuary of Apollo. Among the many other scholars who have contributed their expertise to the Kourion dig are Walter Birkby, Luisa Ferreir Dias, David Grose, Eugene Lane, Rebecca Mersereau, Lucinda Neuru, Stanley Olsen, Ines Vaz Pinto, David Reese, and Donald Sayner. William Dever has offered valuable advice and helped us obtain the support of the American Schools of Oriental Research.

Among our friends on Cyprus who have supported and participated in the dig are J. P. Neophytou of the Cyprus Geological Service; Ino and Kyriakos Nicolaou; Demos Christou, whose excellent guidebook, *Kourion: A Complete Guide,* provided much important information; Christofis Polycarpou; Socrates Savva; and Andreas Giorgiades. Special thanks go to the villagers of Episkopi for their kindness and cooperation.

Other individuals who have helped us in our work at Kourion are Vice-President Melvin George and Chancellor Barbara Uehling of the University of Missouri, Jane and William Biers of the same university, and Norma Kershaw and Bea Riemschneider of *Archaeology* magazine. Unfortunately, we cannot take the space here to mention all the team members who have participated at the Kourion dig, but the following have made especially important contributions: Darice Birge, Hillary Browne, Reuben Bullard, Margaret Craft, Thomas Davis, Caterina Dias, Donald and Nancy Flint, Ron Gardiner, Stephen Glover, Joseph Greene, Carlene Huesgen, John Huffstot, Sian Jones, Frank Koucky, John Leonard, Lena Felix Lopes, Brian McConnell, John MacIsaac, Priscilla Molinari, John Rutherford, Guy and Jan Sanders, Pedro de Santa Barbara, Carol Snow, David Vandenberg, and Terry Weisser.

The historical sections of this book draw on a great variety of sources, ancient and modern, published and unpublished. Among works of general history, the most helpful have been C. Spyridakis's little book *A Brief History of Cyprus* and Sir George Francis Hill's big book, *A History of Cyprus.* The discussion of Count Luigi Palma di Cesnola is indebted to Calvin Tomkins's excellent book about the Metropolitan Museum of Art, *Merchants and Masterpieces,* as well as the count's own masterpiece of humbug, *Cyprus: Its Ancient Cities, Tombs, and Temples.* As a general geographical reference, the Blue Guide to *Cyprus* by Ian Robertson was consulted frequently.

David Soren also wishes to express his gratitude to George McFadden, Robert Scranton, and Joseph Last for laying the groundwork, to the two Elenis and Chrystalla of Episkopi for keeping us so well fed, and to the British forces on Cyprus, who watched over us.

Jamie James wishes to express his gratitude to *Discover* magazine, especially to his chief, Marilyn Minden, for the time generously given him to complete the manuscript of this book.

PART ONE

THE EARTHQUAKE
THAT ENDED
ANTIQUITY

Rumblings

EARLY ON THE MORNING of July 21, A.D. 365, an awe-somely powerful earthquake ripped across the eastern Mediterranean, leveling cities and killing thousands of people. This was one of the great disasters in history. And as sometimes happens, nature was collaborating with history: the monumental tsunamis that rushed through the tidal lands and islands marked, with perfect timing and high drama, a watershed in Western civilization. Indeed, if it had been a film script or a romantic novel, it would be accused of being too perfectly plotted, too thrilling.

Historians are fond of talking about turning points in the development of history, as though such moments can be as easily identified as exit ramps on a highway; yet in this case the

3

phrase fits. The earthquake came just at the moment that pagan Rome, as constituted for nearly a thousand years, was at last unraveling; the moment that Christianity was irrevocably making the transition from being one of numerous moderately successful cults to being the undisputed spiritual and intellectual center of the West. In short, the disaster that destroyed Kourion marks the end of antiquity and the beginning of the Middle Ages. The temples of the pagan empire that collapsed in 365 were not rebuilt; from their rubble were constructed the Christian basilicas and monasteries that preserved the Western tradition during the Dark Ages, protecting it from the barbarous onslaughts of infidels—and launching its share of equally barbarous onslaughts against the same.

Ammianus Marcellinus, the cool, judicious fourth-century Roman historian whose account of his times is one of the most reliable sources available today, describes the quake with terrifying detail:

Just after dawn there were frequent flashes of lightning, and the rumbling of thunder. Then the firm and stable mass of the earth trembled and shook, and the sea withdrew, its waves flowing backward. The sea floor was exposed, revealing fishes and sea creatures stuck fast in the slime. Mountains and valleys that had been hidden in the unplumbed depths since the creation of the world for the first time saw the beams of the sun. Boats were left stranded in these newly created lands, and men wandered fearlessly in the little that remained of the waters, collecting fishes with their bare hands. But then the sea returned with an angry vengeance. As if resentful of its forced retreat, the sea roared and rushed through the seething shallows, dashing through every open space and leveling countless buildings in the cities and wherever else they are to be found, so that amid the mad discord of the elements the altered face of the earth revealed marvelous sights. For the great mass of waters, returning when it was least expected, killed many thousands of men by drowning; and by the swift recoil of the eddying tides a number of ships, after the swelling of the wet element subsided, were found to have been destroyed, and the lifeless bodies of shipwrecked persons lay floating on their backs or on their faces. Other great ships, driven by the mad blasts, landed on the tops of buildings (as happened at Alexandria), and some were driven almost two miles inland, like a Laconian ship which I myself saw in passing near the town of Motho, yawning apart through long decay.

Writing about a century later, the Greek historian Sozomenos talks of what he calls the "famous calamity," a severe earthquake and seismic sea wave, which occurred, he says, in the reign of Julian the Apostate. Some classical scholars now argue cogently that he must be referring to the quake of 365; Julian's reign had ended barely two years before, and Sozomenos confesses that he is not quite sure about the date. In Alexandria the earthquake and subsequent seismic sea wave flooding had such an impact that an annual festival commemorating them was instituted, which continued right up to Sozomenos's own day. His pious explanation for the disaster was that it was the work of God, indignant at the attempts by the pagan Julian to stem the tide of Christianity and to revive worship of the old gods. Whether the quake was indeed the work of a wrathful God must remain a metaphysical question; but the attitude that underlies the claim is relevant, for it demonstrates the pivotal point that the disaster occupies in history, the turning away from the ancien régime, the turning toward Christianity.

We have long known of the quake from the contemporary historical writings, all of which contain descriptions of its tremendous destruction. Before the excavations of my team from the University of Arizona, however, the physical record was virtually nil. In 1984 and 1985, digging at the ancient Greco-

Roman city of Kourion on the southern coast of Cyprus, we discovered the remains of a family, intact, exactly as they had been on that July morning 1,620 years previously when the quake had buried them alive. A little girl, about thirteen years old, and her mule were crushed by stone and masonry in a courtyard. The mule was still tethered by an iron chain to a stone trough, which had been flung by the quake into the wall of the house. Dozens of coins, pots, a marble table, some bronze lamps, and a lampstand were strewn about, thrown violently by the temblor. In an adjoining room, two more bodies, possibly the girl's parents, were found. One was holding a lamp, perhaps having just lit it to go out and see what was the ruckus, what their daughter was doing out in the courtyard at that hour. Nearby, a heavyset laborer had taken refuge under a doorway, which collapsed, crushing his skull and scattering his teeth into the air.

In 1986, in an adjoining habitation, we dug up a family—a man, a woman, and their eighteen-month-old baby. The woman's neck was broken by falling stone and plaster as she held the child to her, trying to protect it with her body. The baby was clinging to her arm. The man, too, was trying to shield his family from the falling stone; his arm covered the baby's back, and his left leg was flung protectively over his wife. He was buried under several six-hundred-pound blocks of stone. Most important of all, the man had a bronze ring inscribed with the chi rho: χρ, transliterated *chr*, the first letters of "Christ" and the earliest symbol for Jesus. Taken as characters of the Latin alphabet, these letters also suggest *pax* (peace), a concept dear to Christians. On either side of the chi rho are inscribed an alpha and an omega, the first and last letters of the Greek alphabet, a reference to Jesus' description of himself in the last chapter of

6

Revelation: "I am Alpha and Omega, the beginning and the end, the first and the last."

This was a Christian family, within the earliest completely preserved Christian community ever discovered.

The Christian Background

IN A.D. 365, AS NOW, the southern coast of Cyprus was far removed from the traditional centers of great worldly power. Kourion had once been a proud city, one of the nine kingdoms of ancient Cyprus; according to Herodotus, she fought side by side with the Greeks in the Persian Wars. That had been many centuries before, however, and the city in the mid-fourth century was a poky little backwater, another obscure corner of the empire.

Yet the empire at this time was becoming more and more a collection of backwaters. Power was rapidly waning in Rome and just beginning to emerge in the new eastern capital, Constantinople. The barbarians were rattling the gate rather ferociously in the north, and bloody civil insurrections blazed everywhere in the East.

As corners of the empire went, however, Cyprus became extraordinarily important. Vital strategically because of its location, the island was a caldron of the conflicting social forces that shaped the beginnings of modern history. The geographical center of the eastern empire, Cyprus was, throughout all of its very ancient history, the meeting place of Europe and the Orient. As one might suspect, these meetings were seldom peaceful.

Culturally, it has probably had more tracks on its soil than any place in the world. When the Greeks colonized the island at the beginning of the first millennium B.C. they found Phoenicians and descendants of Mycenaeans there. Next came the Assyrians and then the Persians, who were displaced by the reconquering Greeks. The great quake occurred during the subsequent Roman rule. To finish the catalogue, the island was later ruled by the Byzantines (with extensive violent meddling by the Arabs), the Frankish Empire, the Venetians, the Genoese, the Turks, and the British. Cyprus became an independent state for the first time in its history in 1960 (unless one includes the brief usurpation in 1184 of the tyrannical Byzantine governor Isaac Komnenos, who styled himself "Emperor of Cyprus" until Richard Coeur de Lion quashed him in 1191). A scant thirteen years later the Turks invaded and occupied the northern part of the island, a partition that continues to exist despite strenuous, passionate objections on the part of Greek Cypriots.

More to the present purpose, Cyprus also serves wonderfully well as a laboratory for observing the clash between paganism and Christianity. The island was famed in antiquity as the birthplace and especial dominion of Aphrodite, that pagan among pagans; and yet at the same time it occupies a position of unique importance in the story of the christianization of the Mediterranean. In Kourion the two religions existed side by side at the time of the quake: an Early Christian basilica had been erected in the city, which was the episcopal seat of one of the most important bishoprics on the island. Meanwhile, the mysteries of Apollo of the Woodlands were practiced just a couple of miles up the road in a beautiful, rustic sanctuary, which appears to have been quite a popular destination for pilgrims. Although there is no evidence of actual hostilities at this time between the pagans and the Christians, things could hardly have been more unstable. In this sense, what was going on in Kourion was a perfect microcosm of an empire that was in a state of permanent instability.

The fourth century was a terrible time to live. Drought and famine, pestilence, religious persecutions, and civil insurrections were the order of the day. Above all, the political order was highly unsettled: at one point, in 308, there were no fewer than six claimants to the emperor's throne. Rome, it seemed, was descending precipitously along the road to decline and fall.

Then there came to power the remarkable Constantine, who radically reorganized the very principles of the empire, and many historians have argued that he single-handedly postponed its dissolution by several centuries. It was during the long, bloody struggle of succession, while Constantine was attempting to consolidate his power, that he had a vision: the night before a great battle, just nine miles north of Rome, he saw a flaming cross in the night sky, emblazoned with the legend *En toutoi nika* (more often rendered in Latin, *In hoc signo vinces,* "In this sign you will conquer"). Then a voice commanded him to inscribe the shields of his men with the chi rho, the monogram of Christ. He did so, and in battle the next day he routed the forces of his rival, whose shields bore the symbol of the Unconquerable Sun, the standard of the pagan cult of Mithras.

He entered the capital the undisputed emperor of the West—
and, nominally at least, a Christian. In 313, shortly after his
accession to the throne, at the urging of his mother—the pious
future saint Helena—Constantine issued the Edict of Milan,
which institutionalized a policy of toleration toward Christianity. Constantine earned his sobriquet "the Great" not by his
great piety but by possessing a rare quality in a leader: he saw
things as they were. He saw that the magnificent imperial edifice constructed by the likes of Augustus and Trajan, which had
withstood such lunatics and wantons as Caligula and Helio-
gabalus, was on the verge of coming apart. Constantine understood that the empire as constituted could not survive; so, with
visionary boldness, he reconstituted it under the sign of the
cross, bringing a new spiritual center to a people who did not
themselves yet know how chaotic things had become.

The common view of Christianity in the fourth century is
that, after three hundred years of cruel imperial persecution,
along came Constantine, who institutionalized the irresistible
trend away from moribund paganism and toward the vital
young religion. That is not actually wrong, but the transition
was a lot bumpier than is usually recognized. In fact, Christianity was one of many popular religions in the Middle East,
which, then as now, was a hotbed of splinter groups and ex-
tremist cults. Christianity itself was very far from being the
brave band of idealists, unified by the strength of their faith,
that popular legend portrays. The religion was torn by ruinous
disputes among groups promulgating conflicting theological
arguments, some of which bore almost no resemblance to the
teachings of Jesus. Schisms, secessions, and heresies were rife.
The early church fathers at times seemed more interested in
excommunicating one another than they were in preaching the
gospel.

Constantine's edict was a dual stroke: he not only Christianized the empire but also temporalized the religion. He was a practical man and had no patience with squabbling bishops. Yet early in his reign, five years after the Edict of Milan, Constantine faced a very deep division in the church—one that threatened to split it down the middle—in the form of the Arian heresy.

About 318 Arius, a priest from Alexandria, began advancing some strange new ideas about the nature of Christ. The French ecclesiastical historian Duchesne describes him thus: "Arius . . . was tall and thin, of melancholy look, and an aspect that showed traces of his austerities. He was known to be an ascetic, as could be seen from his costume—a short tunic without sleeves, under a scarf that served as a cloak. His manner of speaking was gentle; his addresses were persuasive. The consecrated virgins in Alexandria, who were numerous, held him in high esteem." This estimable Arius had the revolutionary notion that the Word, having been created by God, could not be equal to him; and if Jesus was "the Word made flesh," he cannot have been of one substance with God—as traditional Christian theology held—but must actually have been a supernatural being who had visited the Earth, a sort of postpagan demigod. Arianism was very popular, as it provided a way around the concept of the Trinity, always a particularly troublesome one for converts. The ancient mind was much more attuned to the idea of a demigod. According to Eusebius, Constantine's court historian and panegyrist, the controversy caused such "tumult and disorder . . . that the Christian religion afforded a subject of profane merriment to the pagans, even in their theaters."

Constantine impressed on the bishops that to tolerate such a heresy would be far more than simply a dangerous breach of orthodoxy; it would be the first step toward chaos and a serious weakening of the religion's worldly clout. In 325 he ordered a churchwide convocation of bishops to settle the affair. Traveling at Constantine's expense, divines from every part of the empire descended on Bithynian Nicaea, where the emperor exerted considerable pressure on them all to subscribe to the statement that we know as the Nicene Creed. In the end, only two bishops of the several hundred who had been convoked failed to affirm the creed; they were anathematized and exiled. For one brief moment, the last in history, unanimity prevailed in Christendom.

Constantine's rule, like that of many who followed, was Christian more in precept than in example. Late in his reign he had his wife, one of his sons, and a nephew put to the sword; we do not know why. Suffice it to say that he left the good works to his mother, who established churches at the site of Christ's nativity in Bethlehem and over his sepulcher. Here, tradition holds, she found the very cross upon which Christ was crucified, a discovery that was later to have particular significance in Cyprus.

The question of the sincerity of Constantine's conversion is one of those insoluble riddles of history: was he genuinely pious, or a hypocritical politician who cannily saw the way things were going? To support the latter view, much has been made of the fact that he was baptized on his deathbed. This practice, however, was common, especially among worldly men, who postponed the sacrament until the end so that they could face the Kingdom of Heaven with no sins to confess or atone for. Constantine rigorously outlawed sacrifices at the pagan shrines, institutionalized observance of the Sabbath, and even greatly curtailed the imperial cult (the worship of himself as a god), prevalent in the empire's provinces since the reign of

Augustus, the first emperor, and in Rome itself since the time of Caligula. The answer is probably somewhere in the middle: he may have begun somewhat calculatingly, knowing that he needed a bold stroke to unify the empire and to strengthen his own position; then, as his reign prospered and Helena went about the Holy Land discovering relics and establishing churches and convents, he may have come to a sincere conviction in the faith.

At any rate, it was largely through the strength of his own personality that he ensured Christianity's ultimate triumph. Nonetheless, such radical changes take a bit of getting used to: a mere ten years before the Edict of Milan, Christians had been subjected to horrendous mass torture and execution under the persecutions of Diocletian; and anti-Christian sentiment persisted throughout Constantine's reign. It was inevitable that there would be a reaction to the establishment of the religion. This reaction came in the form of Julian the Apostate, who eventually succeeded to the throne in the confusing period after the death of Constantine.

Constantine, who had done so much to unify the empire, divided it in his will among his three sons. Perhaps he knew that an orderly and unified succession would never have worked anyway. Constantine's heirs began to plot against one another almost immediately after their father's death. One son died during an unsuccessful invasion; another proved to be a corrupt tyrant and was assassinated. In 350 the surviving brother, Constantius II, finally reunified the empire under his sole rule as *augustus* (as the emperor was then called). Constantius, however, was a confirmed Arian, which threatened to unravel the whole fabric of his father's Christian empire. Constantius appointed Julian, his scholarly young cousin, to be *caesar*, a secondary post that amounted to "assistant *augustus*," which had been created to dilute the imperial power a bit. Julian proved to be an able military leader and was very well liked by the troops. He was so popular, in fact, that they proclaimed him *augustus*. While Julian and Constantius were preparing to settle the issue on the battlefield in 361, the latter died, naming Julian as his successor.

Upon his accession to the purple, Julian announced his conversion to pagan religion. He reinstituted the old cults (including, naturally, worship of the emperor), and passed edict after edict limiting Christian activities. Julian was very far from being a fanatic or a tyrant; indeed, he was quite a reasonable advocate of paganism as harmonized with Neoplatonism, the school of mystical philosophy based on the writings of Plotinus, which was then popular in the academies. Fortunately for Christianity, he died barely two years after taking the throne. Julian was replaced by Jovian, who reinstituted Christianity and promptly died. Jovian was succeeded in 364 by the brother emperors Valentinian and Valens, the former an orthodox Christian and the latter a fanatical Arian. So Christianity was once again in a very dangerous place, its future far from settled, when the great earthquake occurred, which Sozomenos saw as divine vengeance for the sacrileges of the apostatic empire.

The Church of Cyprus

A S THE PLACE in the Mediterranean that is, more than any other, at once Eastern and Western, Cyprus was ideal for the cultivation of Christianity: for it is important to remember that the early history of Christianity is the story of the way an oriental religion became the most powerful force in the West. St. Paul's very first missionary journey was to Cyprus, where (according to the account in Acts 13:4–13) he made one of his first big conversions, that of Sergius Paulus, the Roman proconsul at Paphos. He accomplished it dramatically, by striking blind Sergius's chief political opponent, an evil man named Bar-jesus. Paul's partner in the early days of his ministry was Barnabas, a Cypriot Jew. Thus Cyprus was only the third place in which the Christian church established a foothold, after Jerusalem and Antioch. Its religious community was recognized

16

from its earliest days as an autocephalous church, one that owed no allegiance to any higher ecclesiastical authority. Other bishoprics, especially that at Antioch, were always trying to annex the Cypriot church, but the islanders clung tenaciously to their religious independence.

The autocephalous status of the Church of Cyprus was finally established in the fifth century by the Third Ecumenical Council at Ephesus. Antioch continued to challenge it, however, until 488, when the archbishop of Cyprus presented to Zeno, Emperor of the Eastern Empire, a copy of the Gospel of St. Matthew. The manuscript, he said, was in St. Barnabas's own handwriting and was found on the apostle's breast in his tomb at Salamis, on the east coast of Cyprus. Furthermore, the Gospel had been placed there by the evangelist St. Mark, who was Barnabas's son-in-law. Zeno was understandably overawed by this apostolic collocation and granted the see of Cyprus perpetual autonomy. He gave its archbishop the distinctions of wearing the purple in official functions and signing documents in red ink, imperial privileges that his modern successors still enjoy.

The Cypriot church got a boost early in the fourth century from Helena, the ever-pilgrimaging mother of Constantine. Sometime after the Edict of Milan, tradition holds, St. Helena went to Jerusalem and discovered the very cross on which Christ was crucified. This event, known to ecclesiastical historians as the Invention of the True Cross, was momentous in the church's history, energizing the faithful in every corner of Christendom. The wood of the cross was greatly coveted by the pious for its miraculous healing power, and bits and pieces were distributed throughout the Holy Land and Europe. On her way home to Constantinople after the invention, Helena's first stop was in Cyprus, where she established numerous churches and gave them all pieces of the cross.

She first founded the monastery of Stavrovouni (Mountain of the Cross) near Larnaca, spectacularly situated on the side of a mountain, called Olympos in classical times, which had formerly been devoted to the mysteries of the cult of Aphrodite. Farther inland, in the hamlet of Kouka, is a little church that enshrines the sawdust that fell from the suppedaneum, or footrest, of the cross, when Helena ordered that it be sawn into pieces. Just a few miles from Kourion, on the Akrotiri Peninsula, she consecrated the monastery of St. Nicholas of the Cats, so called because of the tabby cats she introduced to control a horrifyingly prolific reptile population and, it is said, to provide the monks with inoffensive companionship to divert them from the company of catamites. (In the Middle Ages, St. Nicholas of the Cats became a starred attraction on the itinerary of every tourist to Cyprus, primarily because of the cats' legendary intrepidity. One fifteenth-century Baedeker describes the monastery as it was in those days: "At this place there is a Greek monastery that rears an infinite number of cats, which wage unceasing war with these snakes. It is wonderful to see them, for nearly all are maimed by the snakes; one has lost a nose, another an ear; the skin of one is torn, another is lame; one is blind of one eye, another of both. And it is strange that at the hour for their food, at the sound of the bell, all those scattered in the fields collect in the said monastery. And when they have eaten enough, at the sound of the bell, they all leave together and go to fight the snakes.")

The fourth century was a highly stressful era in Cyprus, one that must have conduced to the power of all religions but especially a religion that offered the consolation of a heavenly reward after the sufferings of this earth. Sufferings there were

18

aplenty. Several natural disasters led up to the great earthquake of 365, including a number of lesser tremors that shook things up a bit (and have made it quite difficult for modern scholars to disentangle their chronology, as we shall see). Cyprus at this time was suffering a precipitous decline in population, caused by plague and a severe drought and resulting famine.

The decline in the island's population had actually begun in the second century, when a man named Artemion had led the Jews there in an insurrection that resulted in widespread massacring of the Gentiles. It was alleged that the entire Gentile population of the city of Salamis was killed, and massacre, of course, led to countermassacre. According to contemporary accounts, by the time the revolt was quelled by imperial forces led by the future emperor Hadrian, the total loss of life had reached the appalling figure of 240,000—equivalent to about 40 percent of the island's population in the present day. Modern historian H. D. Purcell says, "No evidence has been adduced to show this number as exaggerated."

The Cypriots were undoubtedly looking everywhere for some peace, some continuity, a respite from the turbulence of their violent world. Even nature seemed to conspire against them, bringing horrendous earthquakes and seismic sea waves, droughts and famines. At this time in their history Cypriots must have thought that the Beatitudes were written with them specifically in mind. So, when the city of Kourion was rebuilt on top of the rubble from the great quake about twenty years after the disaster, it was as a Christian city. Many of these concerns were plainly on the minds of the people when they built the new city.

For example, in the floor of Kourion's diakonikon, a small building flanking the city's new cathedral wherein the deacons of the bishopric conducted their business (notably the collection of tithes), these quotations from, respectively, Psalms 76:11 and 118:15 and 1 Samuel 16:4 were inscribed: "Vow, and pay unto the Lord your God"; "The voice of rejoicing and salvation is in the tabernacles of the righteous"; and "Comest thou peaceably?" This plaintive interrogatory seems to come straight from the heart of a harried ecclesiastic who had seen many comers who had not done so.

The most important inscriptions at Kourion, the ones that demonstrate vividly the swing from paganism to Christianity, are found in and around the house of a rich man named Eustolios. The practice of lavish public giving had become something of a mania in the late empire; and Eustolios was Kourion's equivalent of J. P. Morgan or John D. Rockefeller. About the turn of the fifth century, Eustolios built beside his mansion what in his day was the most popular and indispensable sort of civic center—a public bath, surrounded by a colonnaded portico that must have provided a lovely view of the sea—and donated it to the city. Lest anyone forget the author of this munificence, he installed the following message, written in the form of elegiac couplets, in black-on-white mosaics in the floor: "Eustolios, having seen that the Kourians, though previously very wealthy, were in abject misery, did not forget the city of his ancestors but first having presented the baths to our city, he was then taking care of Kourion as once did Phoebus [Apollo] and built this cool refuge sheltered from the wind." The primary message conveyed by this verse (after extolling the generosity of citizen Eustolios, of course), is that the worship of Apollo, while in the past, was nonetheless a recent memory.

Elsewhere, the inscriptions and decoration in Eustolios's house are less vainglorious and more pious. Christian imagery abounds, including the well-known symbol of the fish (from the fact that the Greek word for fish, *ichthus*, forms an acronym

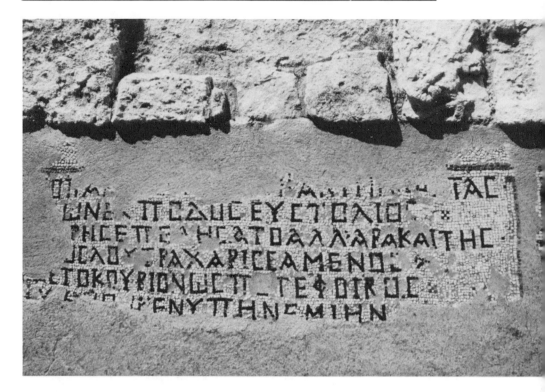

In this inscription in the baths, Eustolios proclaims his patronage of Kourion. From a modern point of view, the key phrase in the verses shows that Apollo's protection of the city is spoken of in the past tense. (NOELLE SOREN)

of Jesus' name—Iesous CHristos, THeou Uios, Soter, the Greek for Jesus Christ, Son of God, Savior), along with the less-familiar representations of the birds of paradise, such as the gray goose, pheasant, partridge, guinea hen, and falcon. An inscription before an entranceway reads, "The sisters Reverence, Temperance, and Obedience to the law [of God] tend the platform and this fragrant hall."

The Christian character of the house is proclaimed in one of

21

This mosaic inscription from the house of Eustolios testifies to the devout Christian belief of the man who built it: "In place of big stones and solid iron, gleaming bronze, and even adamant, this house is girt with the much-venerated signs of Christ." (NOELLE SOREN)

the earliest known public inscriptions on the subject. A perfectly preserved rectangle of white mosaic cubes encloses this message, spelled out with brown cubes: "In place of big stones and solid iron, gleaming bronze, and even adamant, this house is girt with the much-venerated signs of Christ." Composed in a verse form resembling heroic dactylic hexameters and using a Homeric vocabulary, the verse quite self-consciously attempts to integrate this invocation of Christ with the cultural tradition that had existed here previously. The references to stone, iron, bronze, and adamant clearly refer to the pagan religion that preceded Christianity; the versifier seems to be saying that pagan superstition oppresses the soul of man as heavily as do these materials. What gives this passage particular significance is that the same person—perhaps the beneficent Eustolios himself—who wrote about Apollo's protection of the city as though it was not terribly remote in the past, here invokes and venerates the name of Jesus.

The Road to Kourion

THE ROAD that led me to Kourion began in 1959 in the first row of the Surf Cinema in Atlantic City, New Jersey, where, at the age of twelve, I saw Fritz Lang's *The Journey to the Lost City,* in which a handsome German architect-adventurer discovers a buried city. I was utterly captivated by the fantasy world of the movies; and movies about faraway places and fantastic discoveries were the best of all. Grade B movies with archaeological themes like *The Mole People* (John Agar discovers a weird race of Asian troglodytes) and *The Golden Mask* (Van Heflin searches for ancient treasure in Algeria), and of course the many mummy pictures, those masterpieces of frightful make-believe, were my ticket out of the dreary world of my childhood.

But my absolute favorite was *The Journey to the Lost City.* I recall quite distinctly sitting in the Surf Cinema and resolving that, when I grew up, I would discover a buried city of my own. In 1984, when the first human remains started coming up at our excavation at Kourion, I thought of Fritz Lang's adventurer. Somehow, my life had made a complete revolution. Of course, it was a lot easier for him: when he wanted to find his lost city, all he had to do was ask some Indian priests where it was, and they took him right to it. In real life, an archaeologist does not just stumble into a discovery of this magnitude. The journey to my lost city had required years of laborious preparations, spadework both literal and figurative.

My career as an excavation director began not in Cyprus but in Tunisia. In the summer of 1977, I was studying scraps of pottery excavated from the ancient harbor of Roman Carthage by an archaeologist from Harvard named Lawrence Stager, who was then affiliated with the Chicago Oriental Institute. I was all alone in Khereddine. Stager was with his excavation at Dali (classical Idalion), one of the ancient kingdoms of Cyprus; and my wife, Noelle, was with him as the staff artist for the dig.

My quarters in Khereddine were located in a hot, rambling edifice known by the poetic name of the Smithsonian Institution Mediterranean Fish-Sorting Center. In addition to its vital function as a place for fish sorting, the building was also home to the American archaeologists digging in the ruins of Carthage. It was not a cheerful place. My room was especially depressing, as it was also used for storing the ashes and charred bones of babies who were sacrificed by Carthaginians in the fourth century B.C. to appease their gods, who were notoriously cruel and known to be fond of children. The musty, ashy smell of those poor incinerated innocents permeated all my belongings, and bunking amid the grisly sweepings-up of the funeral pyre was really quite dispiriting.

Like most classical archaeologists, I dreamed of having a dig of my own; as Carthage was the place I knew best, I assumed that it would be there. I had lobbied the Tunisian Department of Antiquities long and hard, but the only thing they were willing to give me was a one-acre plot with traces of what might or might not have been a wall built by Emperor Theodosius. It was rather difficult to tell because the site was blanketed by a thick layer of mule dung, the authors of which were tethered in the middle of it. I had cajoled Dartmouth, where I had studied as an undergraduate, and the University of Missouri, where I now worked as a professor, to sponsor the dig, which looked much better in grant applications than it did in life.

Meanwhile, I received a letter from Noelle. She had spoken to Vassos Karageorghis, the director of antiquities in Cyprus, and urged me to come over there to ask him for a dig. I conferred with Larry Stager, who had returned to Carthage to give a lecture, and he seconded the idea. At Stager's suggestion, I asked Karageorghis for a dig at Kourion; among the major classical sites on the island, it was at that time among the least excavated, and it held many interesting possibilities. I devoured what I could find about Cyprus in the library of the Smithsonian Institution Mediterranean Fish-Sorting Center, which was precious little. There was another, more immediate problem than my lack of erudition about Cyprus: I was penniless. Stager lent me two hundred dollars, wrote me a letter of introduction to Karageorghis, and put me on a standby flight to Athens, where I could change for a flight to Larnaca.

Two hundred dollars, it turned out, was exactly enough money for the flight, leaving me without as much as a drachma for a glass of orange juice. I slept on the floor that night at the airport in Athens and ate the leftover bits of other passengers' snacks for my dinner and breakfast. Inauspicious, as Augustus would have said. When I finally made it to Karageorghis's office in Nicosia, I must have cut a rather odd figure: visibly undernourished, I fear, utterly innocent of modern Greek, and quite obviously no great scholar of Cypriot antiquities, there I was boldly asking for permission to excavate one of the most important sites of classical Cyprus. Karageorghis is an adventurous spirit, however, and as I sat in his roastingly hot office, spinning a fantastic tale about all the money I could get for my excavation (in fact, all I had was modest backing from Dartmouth and Mizzou, and they thought they were supporting a dig in Tunisia), I could read plainly in his canny Cypriot face that he was not convinced. He later told me so. Nonetheless, he liked me and I liked him, and after I proved myself to him he gave me the permit.

Now all that remained was for me to have my first glimpse of the place.

The First Campaign

THERE WERE several reasons I settled on Kourion, none of them having to do with ancient earthquakes, about which I knew little. I chose it because there was a large area of Roman and Early Christian ruins that had been at the time but poorly excavated, and underneath them lay earlier cultural levels—Egyptian, Greek, Assyrian—which were almost untouched. It really was two sites: the first, a large city typical of this transitional period, with a forum, a theater, and mosaic baths and houses in full-blown Roman imperial style, spectacularly situated on the edge of a cliff overlooking the Mediterranean. Intermingled with these imperial ruins was an Early Christian cathedral precinct, including a splendid basilica, offertory chapel, baptistry, and bishop's palace, which were erected sometime after the earthquake, incorporating many of the structural features and even statues from their pagan precursors. The other site, two miles up the road to Paphos, was a sanctuary devoted to the cult of Apollo Hylates (Apollo of the Woodlands), comprising a temple, bath, exercise ground (palaestra), and some other cult building that had not been identified.

Kourion was well stocked with the thing that a good archaeologist prizes most: unanswered questions. Many of them were left behind by the last archaeologist who had attempted a long-term, comprehensive excavation at Kourion, an amateur from Philadelphia named George McFadden. He was not a great, or even a good archaeologist, but he did have enthusiasm and (more important, really) lots of money. He dug trenches all over the place and discovered some wonderful things, but they were cursorily drawn, almost never published, and described in only the most abbreviated way in his field diaries. Every now and then, McFadden wrote brief reports for *The Illustrated London News* and the *University of Pennsylvania Museum Bulletin*, but he never published a comprehensive description of his finds.

After McFadden's death, Kourion was neglected, indeed almost forgotten. It may seem incredible that such a promising site, in the possession of a major American university (for Penn owned the land), should be allowed to go untouched for so long. Yet at this time there still flourished the traditional prejudice against Roman civilization, and a particularly strong prejudice against things late Roman, in the archaeological community. Ever since the eighteenth century, when the German classicist Johann Winckelmann first expounded the principles of scientific archaeology, the emphasis had always been on Greece and Greek art; the Romans were widely regarded as heavy-handed copyists with little of their own to offer except a bloody and tyrannical history. I remember Rodney Stuart

Young, the great classical archaeologist at Penn, for example, telling me that he hated Roman art. About the turn of the century there began to be a bit of movement away from this ironclad Grecian hegemony in classical studies: the forward-thinking Alois Riegl, and later George M. A. Hanfmann, the art historian at Harvard, bucked this trend and gave Roman art some serious consideration. Nonetheless, George McFadden was working a somewhat underpopulated field in his excavations at Kourion, and after he died in 1953, the site slowly lapsed into near-total obscurity.

My partner at this time, Diana Buitron of the Walters Art Gallery in Baltimore, and I decided to concentrate in this first campaign at Kourion on the sanctuary of Apollo. The site had become wildly overgrown in the twenty-four years since McFadden's death. While its condition meant that a bit of archaeological housecleaning would be required before we could actually get down to cases, it made the place, the first time I saw it, superbly romantic. It occupies the highest stretch of ground in this part of the island and is one of the most ancient places in all Cyprus. In fact, it was a religious center before the Greeks imported the cult of Apollo to the site in the fifth or fourth century B.C. In the archaic precinct of the sanctuary, votive offerings from the seventh century B.C. have been found that are dedicated simply to "the god," probably a fertility deity with parallels in the religion of the ancient Canaanites. The first reference to Apollo occurs in an inscription on a limestone statue from the fifth century B.C. of a temple boy. Two inscriptions from the fourth century B.C. have been unearthed referring to Apollo Lenaios—Apollo of the Winepress —but by the mid-third century the sanctuary's inscriptions were dedicated to Apollo Hylates, a popular cult throughout Cyprus. Another sanctuary devoted to Apollo Hylates has been found about twenty-five miles to the west, in neighboring Paphos, and inscriptions invoking this woodland god are found as far afield as Kythrea, in the mountains of Kyrenia in the northern part of the island.

By the time of Augustus's reign, the sanctuary of Apollo Hylates at Kourion was a well-known destination for pilgrims, the classical equivalent of a tourist attraction. Strabo, a Greek traveler who wrote an encyclopedic *Geography* of the Mediterranean world, records this tradition associated with the Kourion sanctuary: "The deer, sacred to Apollo, swam to Cyprus from Cilicia, in Asia Minor, to take refuge at Kourion." This information, as fanciful as it may be (it would be a swim of well over 250 miles, requiring the deer to pass up many a likely landfall on the way), is nonetheless interesting and, in view of what we discovered at the sanctuary in 1978, pertinent. Strabo later comments on the extreme holiness of the place: "Those who touched the Altar of Apollo and thus defiled the god were flung into the sea from one of the nearby steep cliffs."

The sanctuary was at its heyday in the second century of the Christian era, the epoch that Gibbon described as the happiest in the history of mankind. It was before the disastrous spell of droughts, famines, earthquakes, and bloody insurrections that ushered in the boom of Christianity in Cyprus, a time when the city of Kourion itself was thriving. Let us imagine what a pilgrim's visit to the sanctuary might have been like.

After the two-mile walk or carriage ride from town (if he were a Kourian), just outside the sanctuary's Kourion gate, the worshiper would enter what amounted to a classical health club. This area comprised, first, the palaestra, an open, colonnaded courtyard devoted to all types of exercise and athletic competitions. In the northern corner was a huge stone jar filled with fresh water for the athletes. (The modern tourist can see this vessel still standing, with the lead pipe that fed it spring-water.) Across the road from the palaestra was a bathhouse, built about A.D. 100, with hot and cold baths. The unheated room, or *frigidarium,* had a small plunge bath.

Then the pilgrim would proceed into the sanctuary itself, entering a little courtyard. Directly across from him, at the opposite end of the court, was the Paphos gate, which led to the main road; on his left was what we now call the south building, a series of rectangular rooms lined with benches and fronted by a colonnaded porch. Across the court from it was another such building, this one positively forested with interior columns. We can only speculate what went on in these two buildings. They may have been dormitories for pilgrims; it is also possible that this whole district was used simply to accommodate waiting worshipers, which would suggest that the sanctuary enjoyed extraordinary popularity. The south building was continually having to be enlarged; there are seven identifiable additions to it. A Greek inscription over one of the central rooms does not help much: it tells us that two of the rooms were constructed by Trajan in the year A.D. 101 for Apollo Hylates and Apollo Caesar (the emperor himself, syncretized with the god through the imperial cult), and that the construction and dedication of these rooms was supervised by a proconsul named Quintus Laberius Justus Cocceius Lepidus.

George McFadden found a foot-high baetyl, or cone-shaped stone sculpture, in one of these rooms. Baetyls stood in for images of a god when the god was too holy to be named or depicted, as Islamic art uses perfect geometric forms to stand in for the perfect and ineffable Allah. The Kourion baetyl is identical to one shown on coins from Paphos as the cult image in the temple to Aphrodite there. That temple has not yet been found, though we do have a vivid description of it by Tacitus, in his narrative of a visit to Cyprus by Titus (later emperor) in A.D. 69: "It is forbidden to pour blood on the altar; the place of sacrifice is served only with prayers and pure flame, and though it stands in the open air it is never wet with rain. The image of the goddess does not bear human shape; it is a rounded mass rising like a cone from a broad base."

When our pilgrim's turn for worship came, he would proceed up a narrow street, lined with shady stoas, in the direction of the holy places. At the foot of the street, just inside the south court, was a *favissa,* a semicircular pit in which McFadden discovered a large number of votive offerings, small terracotta statues, all of them broken up. Apparently, this hole was a sort of sacred garbage dump; when the altars became overcrowded with offerings, the excess were gathered up, perhaps ritually defaced, and deposited here. Across the way a snack bar offered food to pious passersby; perhaps it purveyed the same menu of lamb, roast chicken, potatoes, and hard cheese as do its modern counterparts. McFadden discovered hundreds of cooking vessels here, in what must have been the kitchen.

Then the pilgrim would enter the heart of the sanctuary, the central court. Directly in front of him was the temple of Apollo, but before going there, he would stop to make an offering to the god at the archaic altar, the oldest part of the sanctuary, on the right-hand side of the court. This altar may have been the one Strabo mentioned, the touching of which resulted in one's being hurled from the seaside cliff barely half a mile south of here. In 1935 McFadden found a huge number of offerings at this altar, mostly terracotta figurines dating from the eighth to the fifth centuries B.C. Here we also found the smashed remains of some large terracotta images of bulls with snakes crawling up their legs, as well as two small bull statues, one wrought in gold, the other in silver. Both of them are now

33

These terracotta votive offerings, depicting a stylized tree, a worshiper bringing an animal for sacrifice, and (on page 36) a four-horse chariot group, were recovered at the archaic altar in the sanctuary of Apollo. (JOHN HUFFSTOT)

on exhibit in the Cyprus Museum in Nicosia. Bull imagery in altars was not particularly common in antiquity, but parallels exist, most remarkably, of course, in Minoan Crete, where the practice of bull worship reached a cultic and artistic zenith.

In 1980 we found some highly unusual votive offerings in the archaic-altar precinct that date from the earliest period of the sanctuary (eighth and seventh centuries B.C.), which may offer a clue to the identity of the first deity worshiped here, before the

importation by the Greek colonists of the cult of Apollo. They are terracotta sculptures of human figures holding phalli: one is a woman, holding a pierced phallus against her shoulder, and four others are fragments of hands holding phalli. Some figures found here by the McFadden excavation belong in this group: a man's torso with a strap around the neck, from which depends a phallic object, and another of an erect phallus, which resembles the sort of sculpture used in Dionysiac celebrations.

These figures are unique in the Mediterranean, but they

clearly link Kourion with several fertility cults that flourished in Egypt, Phoenicia, and Greece at this time. One compelling interpretation is that these sculptures depict a Dionysiac phallic procession. Such events were quite well known in antiquity: in the fifth century B.C. Herodotus tells us that they had first been observed in Egypt and Phoenicia and were brought back to Greece by a traveler named Melampus; and a bit later Aristophanes lampoons such processions mounted by the cult of Rural Dionysia. Another early representation of this phenomenon may be found in a sixth-century B.C. Greek vase found at Karnak in Egypt, which shows a satyr carrying a phallus at the head of a Dionysiac procession. By the third century B.C., these festivals had become hugely successful, such as that celebrated by Ptolemy II Philadelphus, in which a multicolored phallus 180 feet long, bound in golden fillets, and with a 9-foot-wide star at its tip, was carried in a cart through the streets of Alexandria.

Undoubtedly, any phallic processions at Kourion would have had a much more modest and becomingly rustic sort of ritual. These votive sculptures are few in number, but they show that the ancient Kourians were aware, at least, of phallic processions on the mainland and may have celebrated a Dionysiac cult of their own. In any case, these offerings bolster the basic assumption that the deities worshiped here before the coming of Apollo were fertility gods, even though their precise function and identity remain a mystery.

By Roman times, this altar was quite an ancient and classical place, and it was here, amid the rubble of the old altar, that we found what was an antique not only to the Romans but to the race that founded this place in the Archaic Period, in the seventh century B.C.: the fragments of an Early Bronze Age vase, a lovely, dark carmine ceramic vessel incised with lime-filled lines, known in archaeologese as Red Polished I South Coast Ware, which dates to about 2000 B.C. It was as remotely antique to the people who consecrated the altar as the late Roman pots of Kourion are to us. There is good reason to believe that some Early Bronze Age tombs at the little settlement known as Phaneromeni, just a couple of miles from Kourion, were looted during the Archaic Period; most likely someone brought this lovely prize to the sanctuary's earliest priests, who thought its antiquity made it a suitable object for dedication to the deity.

To return to our pilgrim: after making his offering at the altar, he would proceed straight ahead to the temple, the Holy of Holies, which towered over everything else in the sanctuary. It was a typical porticoed Greek cult building, constructed of well-finished blocks of limestone, with two rooms, an inner chamber (the *cella*) and a four-columned porch (the *pronaos*). The temple was somewhat elevated and reached by climbing a flight of eleven steps. We believe that this temple (recently reconstructed, in part) was built during the reign of Nero—a notorious big spender whose devotion to Apollo, especially as the protector of poets and strummers of the lyre, is well known. (Nero's own celestial, Apolline vocalizations were said to have caused his listeners, who were forbidden by imperial edict to leave during these performances, to leap to their deaths from the top row of the theater rather than be forced to hear more.) The Neronian temple was erected over the foundations of an earlier, one-room cult building probably dating to the sixth century B.C.

Around the temple and the archaic altar ran a wall of well-dressed local limestone, which would have kept the uninitiated from gazing profanely in on the holy doings. This temenos

Proposed elevation of the facade of the temple of Apollo at Kourion, as it looked by the end of the second century of the Christian era. (ALEXANDRA CORN, JOHN HUFFSTOT, JOHN RUTHERFORD, ROBERT SCRANTON)

39

wall, as it is called, also carried a complete water-distribution system installed about A.D. 60. The sanctuary's cistern, located at the precinct's western edge, was linked with an aqueduct to the north of the city of Kourion.

A Buried Temple

IN BROAD STROKES, that was more or less everything any-one knew about the architecture of the sanctuary of Apollo when I arrived there in 1978. Our first season we were so poor that we could recruit only a dozen scholars and diggers from other Mediterranean sites; they were so exhausted from their other engagements that we were scarcely able to do more than clear up a bit. By the next season, though, we rustled up some cash, including a grant from the National Endowment for the Humanities. We also had time to formulate a historical over-view of the site by deciphering George McFadden's somewhat elliptical diaries and by studying the excellent plans drawn by his architect, Joseph Last.

In 1978 we had discovered a portion of a curved wall com-posed of rubble on the western side of the central court, opposite the archaic altar; when we returned the following summer, we excavated there and hit pay dirt. This bit of wall proved to be all that remained of a circular building, known as a *tholos*, which was unlike anything previously known to classical Mediterranean archaeology. Its existence had never been suspected by McFadden because it was on this spot that the sporty Pennsylvanian had laid out his croquet field. He was apparently devoted to this game, and the field over the ruined *tholos* was flat and wide, and thus ideally suited to his purpose. If he had done a bit of digging here—or for that matter had pounded his wickets in a bit deeper—he would have scooped us.

(Poor George McFadden: after a while, one wearies of pointing out his shortcomings as an archaeologist. In his defense, it ought to be said that he was probably planning to write up a much fuller account of his work when his life was cut short by a tragic, and rather mysterious, accident. A vigorous forty-six, McFadden drowned in the gentle waters of the Mediterranean in a boating accident that was never explained. One does sympathize with him: it is much more fun to dig things up than it is to *write* them up. Nonetheless, he made it devilishly difficult for those of us who came after him at the site.)

The *tholos* was a simple open-air monument, eighteen meters wide, on an artificially elevated stretch of earth surrounded by a parklike precinct. Within its walls was a paved circular walk, and dug into the ground were seven pits, each almost a meter deep and wide. It has been suggested that these pits might have served as homes to sacred serpents, as was the case in the *tholos* at Epidaurus. Diana Buitron and I hypothesized that these pits were planters for trees. Date palm trees, particularly, are sacred to Apollo. According to Charles Miksicek, our palaeoethnobotanist (a specialist who studies how plants were cultivated in antiquity), the date palm's smallish root system could have survived in these holes. Geologist Reuben Bullard has made a study of the pits and found that the caliche bedrock shows traces of disturbance by major plant action. This phenomenon is known as plant wedging. There exist models for this rock-cut plantation concept in classical Greece: similar rock pits, dating to the turn of the fourth century B.C., have been found at the agora in Colonus, in the Asklepieion north of the temple of Apollo at Corinth, and as a part of the terracing alongside the Hephaisteion in Athens.

One of the most perplexing and fascinating aspects of the *tholos*, as always with classical cult structures, is the question of what went on there. The ancients called their sacred rituals mysteries, and that is exactly what they were and continue to be, for the most part. While reams of miscellaneous writings pertaining to religious practices have survived, they constitute a confusing jumble. There existed no equivalent to the Book of Common Prayer for the cults of Apollo, and the situation is even worse for the vestiges of the pre-Apolline cult. One will find not the smallest measure of the orthodoxy that we moderns expect from a religion. Communications were more difficult in general, and ritual activities varied greatly from place to place. Unless one is lucky enough to have a manuscript associated with a particular temple (which we do not in this instance), one may only indulge in informed speculation as to what the mysteries involved.

Nonetheless, a glimpse into the Apolline ritual at Kourion may be afforded by some charming Cypriot terracotta statuary groups of celebrants dancing to the accompaniment of pipes and tambourines. Another terracotta group, of some initiates holding hands as they dance around a palm tree, which had been influential in our original tendency to the point of view that ritual activity involving sacred trees went on at Kourion,

43

turned out to be a fake. The different pieces of the group were apparently glued together at an unknown time by an unknown hoaxer. But this fraud in no way diminishes the tree theory, for there is plenty of authentic evidence in existing terracottas to support it. Also, there is at Kourion an inscription that describes worshipers at Kourion in the second century dancing around an altar in honor of Antinous, Emperor Hadrian's favorite, who was venerated by cults throughout the Mediterranean for his Apollo-like good looks. Furthermore, in view of some magic rituals associated with trees that have continued to the present day in Cyprus, it makes sense to suppose that the trees themselves may have been part of the mysteries of the *tholos*.

Let us, then, hypothesize an ecstatic procession of worshipers, holding hands or playing music around the paved walkway, perhaps hanging propitiatory gifts from the sacred trees to ward off evil. Something like a large baetyl may have been at the center. In the beginning, these rites may have been performed in the open air on an elevated holy precinct, and then, as the authority of the cult at Kourion grew, the *tholos* was built to formalize the ritual and to screen these holy goings-on from the hoi polloi. Of course, there is no reason to limit our hypothesis to these elements—free-standing statuary might certainly have been incorporated into the temple—but the trees would have provided a focus, symbolizing the power and fecundity of the vegetation deity who dominated the sanctuary before it came to be associated with Apollo.

In 1979 an archaeologist named Georges Roux published an important article about the Pythion, a sanctuary consecrated to Apollo on the Greek island of Delos, which appears to be quite similar to our conception of the Kourion *tholos*. The sanctuary at Delos had an interior colonnade enclosing a *thalamos*, or open court, with a sacred palm tree marking the birthplace of

This terebinth tree in modern Paphos, near Kourion, has been trans-formed into a "rag tree": rags and articles of clothing from sick people are hung here and dedicated to the Virgin Mary or to St. Solomoni, a healing saint. This practice may be a syncretistic survival of nature worship, including sacred trees, which might have gone on at the sanctu-ary of Apollo. (JOHN HUFFSTOT)

Apollo. The altar area was marked off with goat horns and reserved for ritual ring dancing around a small *tholos*, which, like the one at Kourion, was preserved into the Roman period.

The veneration of sacred trees is something that continues to be practiced in Cyprus, and it is tempting to view these magical rites as a syncretistic survival of the mysteries of the cult of Apollo. When someone is sick, an article of his clothing or his

45

handkerchief is tied to the tree as an appeal to the Virgin or to a healing saint, such as St. Panteleimon (who closely resembles Asklepios, the pagan god of health) or St. Solomoni. They are called rag trees, and one existed in Episkopi, the modern village nearest to ancient Kourion, until 1980, when it was cut down at the order of the church, which wanted to stamp out this superstitious practice. In fact, it was just one block from our dig headquarters in George McFadden's stone house, which now houses the Kourion Museum. Next to the tree was a crudely built modern shrine dedicated to the Virgin and St. Spyridon, a fourth-century Cypriot bishop who was one of the leading church fathers summoned to Nicaea by Constantine for the first ecumenical council. Spyridon worked wonderful miracles —he struck liars blind and turned the teeth of uncharitable people yellow—and in Episkopi he, in tandem with the Virgin, is the great healer and thaumaturge.

Is it too fanciful to connect this modern practice of the rag tree with the mysteries of Apollo at the *tholos* in the Kourion sanctuary? One is struck everywhere in Cyprus with the number of ancient traditions that have survived, especially in liturgical rites, however much the Church of Cyprus officially frowns on such crypto-paganisms. It is more than a flippancy to say that there is no reason *not* to think so; tradition is always persuasive, absent some definite reason to disbelieve it. It is at least reasonable to look at a modern rag tree—an open-air shrine in a traditionally holy place, hung with talismans—and see the latest manifestation of a rite that goes back to the island's earliest local nature worship, which adapted itself to the introduction of the Greek cults; and then, when Christianity came along, it found a place there, too.

The Rock-Cut Channels

YET ANOTHER MYSTERY is presented by the sanctuary's network of rock-cut channels. Carved firmly into
the site's caliche bedrock, these channels are found in the area
east of the temple of Apollo, between the *tholos* and the central
court, near the cistern on the western edge of the complex, and
in the street inside the Paphos gate—in short, all over the place.
The channels vary in depth and complexity but sometimes line
up in organized patterns, and many of them hug the temenos
wall or frame the temple of Apollo. No one knows what to
make of them, though everyone has a theory. Hypotheses range
from the merely functional to the bizarre and mystical. We
have settled on the same explanation here as for the pits in the
tholos: that they were a locus for ritual horticulture and land-
scaping.

George McFadden found the first one, which runs right under the steps of the temple and enters it at a right angle. He did not publish the finding and hypothesized in his field diaries that it might be connected with water drainage. A more romantic interpretation is taken by Rupert Gunnis in his 1936 guidebook to Cyprus: "The original cave over which the temple was built can, however, still be seen; it faces southeast, and was connected with the temple itself by a passage running east and west, perhaps a natural vault in the rock."

Gunnis finds support for the cave theory in a passage from Pausanias, a writer of the second century of the Christian era whose account of his travels in Greece was one of the first guidebooks. Pausanias describes a cult of Apollo in a place called Hylai, tantalizingly close to the Hylates of this sanctuary (it is the same word really), located in Magnesia, in Greek Asia Minor: "Here there is a cave dedicated to Apollo, not very impressive as far as its size is concerned, but having an extremely old statue of Apollo, which provides strength for every task. The holy men of the god leap from precipitous cliffs and high rocks and, ripping up huge trees by the roots, they make their way down the narrowest paths with their loads." Many local inhabitants, always worth listening to in such cases, also subscribe to this notion of the oracular "cave." So many of these channels have been discovered in the past fifty years, however, that this theory now seems rather improbable, as it would leave the holy men of the god with little else to do except burrow in these tiny grooves in the rock.

Some rather more utilitarian explanations include the obvious suggestion, put forward by McFadden, that they were used for water drainage. But they have no issue, nor are they connected with the cistern. Also, geologist Frank Koucky examined some of the channels microscopically and found no trace of the sorts of water-borne detritus that one would expect were that the case. Another suggestion is that the channels may have served as oracular crawl spaces for the temple's holy men, as at Apollo's temple at Corinth. Yet another theory was that they might have been quarries for the construction of the temenos wall, but that one is easily disproved by the fact that the channels and the wall are not contemporary with each other.

That leaves our theory—that the channels, like the pits in the *tholos,* served as planters for trees sacred to this god, whose very name invokes the woodlands. There is evidence everywhere in Cyprus that the ancient inhabitants were dedicated horticulturists, as indeed was almost everyone in classical times. Many of the channels still serve that purpose today: just east of the Paphos gate is a channel that contains quite a luxuriant little orchard of pomegranate trees; and along the temenos wall, another is home to carob trees and some large pistachio shrubs. The orderliness of the patterns in which the channels are laid out suggests that they were ornamental and helped to define the space in the sanctuary. This theory also explains why the channels would vary so much in dimensions, for they would have been custom-made for each tree or group of bushes brought to the site.

This view also provides a plausible explanation of the whole precinct as a coherently designed religious retreat, the landscape beautifully integrated with the architecture. Furthermore, we have found some statuettes of deer in the west precinct, the area surrounding the *tholos,* suggesting that deer, which were plentiful in this part of the island, may have been kept by the priests as part of the cultic ambience. Apollo had powers to charm the beasts of the forest with the beautiful tones of his lyre, and therefore a deer sanctuary would have been appropriate.

The idea that the area around the *tholos* might have served as a protected refuge for such woodland animals—in fact as a sort of holy zoo—finds support in the writings of Aelian, a thoroughly Atticized third-century rhetorician from the ancient Italian city of Praeneste. In his odd little book of fables, *The Ways of the Animals*, he describes the mystical-natural lore associated with the sanctuary of Apollo at Kourion: "On Kourias, when the deer, of which there are a great number and many hunters keen in pursuit of them, take refuge in the Sanctuary of Apollo there (its grove is very large), the hounds bay at them but don't dare to approach. But the deer in a body graze undeterred and without fear, and by some mysterious instinct trust to the god for their safety."

Sacred groves, whether cultivated as at Kourion or occurring naturally, were commonplace in the ancient world; and their use as a wildlife refuge or as a sacred zoo was widespread. We have a venerable and pedigreed literary source that describes just such a place—strikingly close to our vision of the sanctuary at Kourion—in the *Anabasis* of Xenophon. His campaigns in the East over, the old soldier bought an estate at Skillous, near Olympia. After consulting an oracle about a good location, Xenophon dedicated a shrine to Artemis comprising a temple, an altar, a grove of cultivated fruit trees, and a refuge for wild animals.

In *The Ways of the Animals*, Aelian describes some other classical shrines populated by fabulous animals. For example, at the sacred grove of the temple consecrated to Hephaistos at Mount Aetna, there were one thousand sacred dogs that had mysterious powers of comprehending human nature—they welcomed morally upright visitors, turned away licentious people, and bit anyone who had committed a crime. At Apollo's sanctuary in Epirus, Greece, was a grove given over to snakes that were kept as pets for the god. Strabo tells us that in the groves of Hera and Artemis on the Adriatic wild deer mingled safely with wolves and were unmolested by hunting dogs. Tourists could pet them. Finally, and charmingly, according to Philostratos, in a grove on Leuke Island in the Black Sea Achilles used the birds as groundskeepers: they watered the holy trees with drops of water they collected on their feathers.

All of these tales attest that the idea of an ancient holy zoo is not so improbable. Classicists are sometimes asked why we cite such interminable catalogues of literary references (the foregoing is but a tiny sliver of the scholarly treatment of sacred groves recently undertaken by Darice Birge of Columbia University) and the answer is that the ancients were so literary themselves. Writers like Xenophon were quite popular, and a book like the *Anabasis*, which was his account of the wanderings of the Ten Thousand after the debacle of the Persian Wars, was familiar to every educated person. Where firsthand accounts are very scanty, as at Kourion, one must rely on educated guesses to form an accurate picture of life at a particular site. And the literature that would have been known to the people of the place is one of the best methods, and in some cases the only method, we have for educating our guesses.

Another highly educated guess we made that season about where we might find a little row of stones and what they might mean, proved to be our biggest find of the summer.

Unearthing the Earthquake

A N ARCHAEOLOGIST, to get the most out of what are often rather slender materials, must try to think like a detective. And as in the Sherlock Holmes tale in which the master sleuth finds the missing letter in plain view, in the letter file, sometimes the most important information may be derived from objects lying about openly. As we were preparing for the 1979 campaign, one of the tools we had at our disposal was an extensive file of photographs of the Kourion site in the collection of the University of Pennsylvania Museum. These pictures, most of them taken in the 1930s by the McFadden team, had been carefully organized by Roger Edwards, a curator at the Penn museum. The photo file was supplemented by the carefully detailed architectural drawings of Joseph Last.

As I studied these fifty-year-old pictures of the site, I noticed something that proved to be very important: behind the temple of Apollo and to the east of it were some large stone blocks that had since been covered with topsoil and vegetation. Something about the way they were situated arrested my eye. They appeared not to be arranged randomly, or as if they had been left that way by vandals, but rather as if they had *fallen* that way. That was the beginning of a long train of thought about earthquakes in Cyprus during the late empire.

I knew, of course, that Kourion had been racked by earthquakes in the fourth century, and that it was generally supposed that a quake had finally destroyed the sanctuary. Different hypotheses had fixed the date for the fatal temblor at 321, 332, 342, and 345. If the stones still lay as they had fallen from the earthquake—perhaps the same disaster that had felled the city of Kourion two miles away—then we might be able to study the blocks and actually reconstruct the back wall. Through a bit of logical extrapolation, we could then, for the first time, have an accurate idea of what a Roman Cypriot temple of the Neronian era looked like. We might even be able to rebuild it.

It was a big *if*, however: there was no particular reason to think that McFadden would have left the stones in situ. And even if McFadden had left things as he found them, fifty years —and countless tourists, amateur archaeologists, and just curious folk—had passed by since those photographs were taken and Joseph Last made his drawings. It would have looked like a perfectly dull pile of rocks to most people, and it seemed all too likely that they had been disturbed. At the same time, the fact that the blocks weighed hundreds of pounds argued in favor of their having been left as they were.

It was not difficult to excavate the topsoil and rainwash that had built up over the area behind the temple, and one by one they emerged from the earth. They were intact, lined up in

53

delightfully orderly rows, just as they had been when they had formed courses of the temple wall—just as they had been when the earthquake toppled them. That was the first of many moments of almost eerie intimacy with ancient Kourion: true, it is difficult to get too sentimental over a stone wall, but there was a sense of immediacy, of direct and unimpeded connection with the ancient residents of this place, in the certainty that this part of their holiest place was still just exactly as it had been at the moment that their world tumbled.

Now we had a new problem: how to get a good aerial-view photograph of the blocks, which is essential for a serviceable schematic drawing. Also, once you begin to remove objects from a site, unless you have some good photographs, afterward you will never know what the place looked like before you started messing around with it. The extent of the fallen stones made it necessary to get twenty-five feet above them to shoot. This height was beyond the reach of the biggest stepladders in Cyprus (ladders do not really work, anyway, because they get into the pictures so much themselves), and a cherry picker would have destroyed too much potentially excavatable terrain —even had one been available, which it was not. We thought about trying to charm the use of a helicopter out of the Royal Air Force, which has a base scarcely three miles from the sanctuary, but a helicopter would not be able to hover any lower than seventy feet from the ground, and the wind would have kicked up so much dust in the summer drought that it would have made the photographs useless.

Our architect, Jack Rutherford, solved the problem with a recently developed item known as the Whittlesey Bipod. The Whittleseys are a husband-and-wife team of pioneers in the fairly recondite field of archaeological photography. Many of their devices have involved aerial balloons, manned and unmanned, but the bipod is a wonderfully simple gadget, consisting of two telescoped aluminum legs, extensible to a height of twenty-five feet (conveniently enough), with guidewires to steady it. The thing can be easily raised into the air, like a giant geometer's compass, forming an upside-down V (or, to be classical about it, a lambda); then the camera is raised to the crotch by a pulley and fired by remote control.

After we had photographed the stones, we were able to begin examining them. We soon realized that we were looking at the top part of the temple's rear wall: the violent pulse of the earthquake had sheared the upper portion of the building right off and thrown it here, like a machete cutting through tall grass. We began hunting around the area for other, randomly fallen pieces of the temple, and turned up a good many. These, combined with blocks unearthed previously by Robert Scranton, an architectural historian from the University of Chicago who had come out of retirement to join our expedition, were enough to reconstruct the whole building. We had a capital from the front, pilasters from the rear, and bits and pieces of the pediment and cornices.

Especially valuable was the corner cornice block. Although somewhat worn and weather-beaten, it showed the decorative treatment of the upper course of the temple on both the front and the sides, as well as the pitch of the roof. It was rather like getting a key word in a crossword, which then enables you to solve the rest of the puzzle—or, a closer analogue, finding the corner piece of a jigsaw puzzle, except in this case we did not have the boxtop to show us how the thing was supposed to look in the end.

Thus began in earnest our earthquake detective story. From the drawings and photographs, both old and new, it was clear that the blocks had fallen to the north and east; that meant that the shock wave of the temblor, the vector that had destroyed the temple, may have originated in the opposite direction, the southwest.

Our geologists, Reuben Bullard and Frank Koucky, showed me how to estimate the magnitude of earthquakes from simple observation of the damage, a skill that was going to prove increasingly useful as our excavation became more and more seismically oriented. The yardstick for these empirical measurements is called the Modified Mercalli Scale, which was used long before more sophisticated electronic and mechanical methods were invented and is still employed on Cyprus. It is an ascending scale, from zero to twelve. If windows crack and relatively heavy objects like pots are thrown from shelves, the temblor is rated at four or five; a reading of twelve indicates total devastation, with great fissures opening in the earth, large buildings leveled, and much loss of life. Bullard and Koucky tentatively gave the quake that destroyed Kourion an eleven. The evidence for such a highly rated quake included the hurling of large stone blocks from the temple of Apollo, displacements of earth of more than a yard in a house in Kourion, and a reference in a field diary from the McFadden excavation to some human victims that had been found. The geologists hypothesized that the epicenter must have been quite near, perhaps little more than twenty-five miles away.

At this point it was necessary to enlarge the quest beyond Kourion and take in all of Cyprus. I began by enlisting the aid of J. P. Neophytou, a Cypriot geophysicist who had dedicated his life to the study of seismic activity on this island. He was quite happy at our interest in his findings and immediately confirmed the working hypothesis of Koucky and Bullard: twenty-five to thirty miles southwest of Kourion was indeed an extremely volatile earthquake zone. It was just here that two great land masses, the African and European plates, were joined.

When I was an undergraduate, just twelve years before, plate tectonics was quite a wild and woolly idea according to official geology. My professor at Dartmouth openly ridiculed it in class, as I recall. Now, however, it is widely accepted. Neophytou simplified it for me: the earth's crust contains very deep fissures, which may reach down as far as sixty miles into the planet's surface and which divide it into great crustal masses floating on top of a sea of magma, or molten rock. These huge crusts, or plates, collide into one another; one plate may ride up over another, forcing it down into the magma, in a process known as subduction. Sudden shifts of this type create earthquakes and (if they occur at sea) tsunamis.

To find the epicenter of the temblor and to begin trying to date the event—generally to enlarge the geological context—I started looking into the contemporaneous earthquake at Paphos, the ancient city that lies about twenty-five miles to the west of Kourion. One thing was clear: the quake that leveled Kourion ought to have wreaked terrible damage at Paphos. Then I had an idea: we knew the direction in which the debris at Kourion tended to fall, to the north and east; and I thought that if we went to Paphos and were able to determine in which direction things generally had fallen there, we would then be able to pinpoint the epicenter through the traditional surveyor's process of triangulation.

In Paphos I examined earthquake debris at the newly discovered house of Herakles and found that the walls of the building had fallen generally to the north and *west*; again, the damage on the Modified Mercalli Scale was observed to be between nine and twelve. I also toured the excavations being carried out by a team of Polish archaeologists at the villa of Theseus (so called because of the exquisite mosaic representation of that hero in the labyrinth, among the finest late Roman mosaics extant). Judging by its splendor, the villa was probably the official residence of the Roman governor of Cyprus. Here the Poles had found a nearly complete earthenware pot almost identical to one we found in Kourion. The Paphos pot appeared, from its form, composition, completeness, and the way it had fractured, to be a certifiable relic of our earthquake. This discovery gave weight to the thesis that the Paphos quake and the Kourion quake were one and the same. Again, we found quakefall tending toward the northwest. I reasoned that the epicenter must have been somewhere midway between Paphos and Kourion. We could draw two vectors on a map, showing the shock wave's angles of approach to the two sites, and where they intersected must be (more or less) the epicenter.

Of course, it was not quite that simple, but it almost was. Neophytou tentatively fixes the coordinates of the epicenter at a spot, still seismically active, offshore of Paphos about twenty miles south of Petra tou Romiou (Aphrodite's Rock), a great rock on the coast by the ancient city of Palea Paphos, where, as everyone knows, Aphrodite was born amid the sea foam and then transported to shore on a shell borne aloft by Zephyr. (Her cult there, until it was finally shut down by Emperor Theodosius, was reputed to be the most licentious in all antiquity; according to the fourteenth-century tattletale Ludolf von Suchem, here "all ladies and damsels before their betrothal yielded themselves to men; for in Cyprus above all lands men are by nature most luxurious.") Reuben Bullard dissents, saying that if the epicenter were that close, the damage would have been even more severe than it was. He believes that the source was a bit farther south, though he will not commit himself to precise coordinates.

Dating the disaster proved to be a more stubborn problem. There was much confusion in the published scholarship as to the exact date of the Kourion–Paphos quake, but there seemed to exist a conspiratorial unanimity that it occurred in the early part of the fourth century. All of the guidebooks, all of the geophysical studies stated that the Paphos quake took place between 332 and 345. Despite these claims, I was arriving at a wholly new concept for dating the disaster. It began while I was disentangling the notes of McFadden and his young assistant, Penn scholar J. F. Daniel. Like his boss, Daniel died quite young, while working on a dig in Turkey; in his mid-thirties and apparently in hearty good health, he dropped dead of a heart attack. As I digested the data that the geologists were coming up with, I became convinced that the quake was much later than anyone had ever suggested—in fact, that it was the megaquake described by Ammianus, Sozomenos, and the rest.

The most compelling clue in this direction came from the testimony of the coins that were found at the site: coins, with pots and clay oil lamps, are the archaeologist's traditional and still most reliable timepieces. The McFadden expedition had discovered many coins, but they had been listed without any mention of where they had been found, which made it somewhat more difficult to synthesize from them the information I was particularly seeking. As I pored over Daniel's notebooks, however, a pattern emerged: there were coins issued up through the joint emperorship of the brothers Valens and Valentinian I, but no coins from the rule of Gratian, the son of Valentinian, who made him co-*augustus* in 367. Of course, that constituted nothing more than the grounds for a hunch about how to date the earthquake that brought down Kourion. Daniel's notes were interesting but nothing more at this point, because we could not be sure that the findings were complete or untampered with. In the meantime, however, our literary spadework, which is quite as important as the literal type, was starting to pay off.

The Literary Evidence

A S ARCHAEOLOGY becomes more and more scientifically
oriented, bringing in laboratory technicians of every
stripe, it is gratifying that classical scholarship of the old-fash-
ioned sort is still essential to our work. No one has yet figured
out how to teach a computer to analyze literature, which is an
utterly human activity, full of ambiguities and questions that
cannot be answered to everyone's, or indeed at times to anyone's, satisfaction. Nonetheless, the literary evidence is crucial
to our dating of the Kourion quake, and it is still a controver-
sial issue.

Ammianus Marcellinus's vivid description of the great quake
of July 21, 365, appears in the opening pages of this book; as a
reliable eyewitness account, certainly, it cannot be bettered.
Likewise, Sozomenos's description of what he calls "*the* calam-

ity at Alexandria," also mentioned before, may quite reasonably be identified with Ammianus's disaster; indeed, a later editor of Sozomenos's writings, one Henricus Valesius, even claims that the festival of remembrance of *the* calamity, held every year at Alexandria, may be dated precisely to July 21.

Of course, these texts were general works of history that in no way treat Kourion directly. The key to using such literary sources is to construct a tissue of logical inferences that will hold up to independent scrutiny: in other words, to publication and review by other scholars. In our case, this work has been done by Richard C. Jensen, a classics scholar whose interpretations of the fourth-century sources have served us well in the Kourion dig and also provide a good textbook case of how to bend rather slim literary pickings to one's service.

There are several other instances in which fourth-century histories refer to earthquakes very similar to Ammianus's, which are in all likelihood the same one. The uninitiated reader might think that the brevity of these accounts is evidence that the writer does not consider the event to be terribly important. Jensen, however, points out that this brief treatment "in no way suggests that the events were less significant, but rather reflects the spare, stripped style of these particular authors"; merely to be mentioned in their works suggests importance. From this fact may be derived one of the basic laws of practical classical studies: Know thy source.

According to the fifth-century historian Socrates Scholasticus (whose name, at least, is impressive), the first year of the rule of Valens and Valentinian—that is, 365—was marked by a tremendous earthquake, with this result: "The sea changed its familiar boundaries; for in some places the quaking was so severe that places where previously people walked they now could sail. In other places the sea retreated so far that [the bottom] was found to be dry. And this happened in the first administration of the two rulers." Socrates is not very clear: one cannot be sure whether he means that the coastline changed permanently, always a possibility in a big earthquake, or whether this is a somewhat garbled account of a tsunami based on accurate accounts like that of Ammianus, who described that event, it will be recalled, thus: "The sea floor was exposed, revealing fishes and sea creatures stuck fast in the slime. Mountains and valleys that had been hidden in the unplumbed depths since the creation of the world for the first time saw the beams of the sun."

Another fifth-century historian, Orosius, reports a "world"-wide seismic disaster in the early years of the reign of Valens and Valentinian, mixed in with other events, including the suppression of a revolutionary troublemaker named Procopius: "Valentinian killed Procopius the tyrant and many of his followers afterwards. An earthquake occurring throughout the world so shook and stirred the sea that in neighboring parts of the flatlands many cities are said to have perished, shaken and uprooted when the sea poured back." In analyzing this passage, again, one must do a bit of mind-reading. Procopius was not put to death until 366, but it is not at all clear that Orosius's account intends to be strictly chronological. Perhaps he is merely coupling the two occurrences (as indeed had Socrates Scholasticus), narrating two events that happened at more or less the same time, but not necessarily in order. Were that the case, one might reasonably propose that the disastrous earthquake he describes is the same one Ammianus wrote about as having occurred in the year 365.

Further light was shed by some passages in the writings of St. Jerome, the author of the Vulgate and one of the Four Doctors of the Church. In his *Chronica*, a continuation of the annals

63

of Eusebius, Constantine's court historian, he describes the principal events of the second year of Valens and Valentinian's reign: "When an earthquake occurred throughout the world, the sea swamped the coastline and destroyed unnumbered nations and cities of Sicily and many [other] islands. Procopius, who had made himself tyrant of Constantinople, was destroyed in Phrygia Salutaris, and many of the Procopian party were proscribed and slain." Once again the death of Procopius and the great earthquake are mentioned in tandem, this time in the correct chronological order if we are indeed dealing with Ammianus's quake.

The problem here is that the second year of Valens and Valentinian's rule was 366. One must always bear in mind that classical documents were copied by hand over and over again, and many errors creep into the literature. Jerome's editor, and Jensen, think that the scribe may have misnumbered the entries, accidentally marking the last paragraph of 365, the brother emperors' first year, as the first entry in 366. Jensen makes an excellent point about a scholar's constant need for vigilance when dealing with these documents, in what is actually a footnote about a footnote:

> We must not be too hard on *incauti amanuenses* [careless scribes]; sooner or later we are all guilty. By one of those poignantly instructive accidents that the gods of scholarship arrange for all of us, the same . . . note [that asserts this clerical error in the Jerome manuscript] claims, *"Nihil dubium, quin terramotus ille idem sit, quem Ammianus lib. XXIV describit, consule Valentiniano primo cum fratre Valente."* "No doubt this is the same earthquake that Ammianus describes in Book XXIV, during the first consulship of Valentinian with his brother Valens." The correct number is XXVI.

Jerome's mention of Sicily, nearly a thousand miles from the postulated epicenter, is especially instructive, as it demonstrates the tremendous power of the earthquake and tsunami. That the quake should have been felt as far away as Sicily is by no means surprising for a seismic event of this magnitude; in the 1946 earthquake in Alaska, tsunamis 55 feet high swept over the Hawaiian Islands, 2,300 miles away. Thus, far from making the identification with Ammianus's quake less likely, this mention of Sicily actually strengthens the case.

Another important passage from Jerome occurs in a little hagiography he wrote of St. Hilarion, an obscure Palestinian anchorite. Writing about A.D. 380, at the latest 391, Jerome tells us that Hilarion was at Epidaurus in Dalmatia when an earthquake was felt there, a disaster that affected the entire world at some time after the death of Julian the Apostate. According to his biographer, the aged saint went down to the shore and stopped a seismic sea wave from inundating the place. The exact date of this disaster is a bit of a problem: Jerome only tells us that it was *post mortem Iuliani*, after Julian's death, which occurred in 363. "After the death of Jovian," Julian's successor who died in 364, would fit much better if one were trying to make a case for identifying this event with Ammianus's quake (which we are not). Again, it is possible that a scribe's error has crept in; Jerome's editor suggests that *Iuliani* ought to be read as *Ioviani*. It would not be the first time that the two emperors were confused: after the death of Julian, his soldiers, hearing the cry of "Iovianus Augustus" thought that they were hearing "Iulianus Augustus" and believed that Julian had recovered.

Nevertheless, in this case one may take Jerome at his word and assume that he is writing about an entirely different earthquake, occurring in 363 or 364. It is rather unlikely that an earthquake originating southwest of Cyprus could direct a tsunami against Epidaurus. These destructive seismic sea waves must travel in straight lines, and the entire Balkan Peninsula intervenes between the epicenter of our postulated megaquake and the city of Epidaurus, halfway up the Adriatic.

If all of the foregoing seems to be a trifle overwrought, carefully pointing out a possible interpretation only to knock it straight down, it serves as a good illustration of the kind of preventive argumentation that a scholar must undertake. At times it is a bit convoluted, but it ultimately saves time to disarm your adversary. And the more careful one is to examine all of the possibilities, the more likely one is to arrive at a convincing and correct reading.

Immediately after his spectacular performance at Epidaurus, Hilarion left for Paphos, where, Jerome tells us, he entertained visitors from many Cypriot cities, including Salamis, Lapithos, and Kourion. No mention is made of any disasters having occurred there, which would be most unusual if the enormous earthquake that leveled Kourion had just occurred a few months before. Indeed, Jerome gives us a good clue, when he writes *"Paphum, urbem Cypri nobilem carminibus poetarum, quae frequenter terrae motu lapsa* nunc [our emphasis] *ruinam tantum vestigiis, quid olim fuerit, ostendit,"* which may be translated, "Paphos, a city of Cyprus celebrated in the songs of poets, which, having been destroyed frequently by earthquakes, *now* shows only in traces a ruin of what it once was."

The Latin is not Jerome's loveliest work, but what he says is plain enough: Paphos has by now (meaning when Jerome was writing, about 380 or after) been completely destroyed by earthquakes; yet when St. Hilarion visited Paphos it was still "what it once was." Unfortunately, Jerome does not state specifically when the saint arrived in Aphrodite's city, but the clear inference is that it was immediately after the quake occurring *post mortem Iuliani,* in 363 or 364. Jerome implies, as we have seen, that Paphos at this time was still prosperous and sound; therefore, logically, the city's destruction must have occurred after Julian's death in 363 and before Jerome was writing, about 380 at the earliest. The best explanation that springs to mind, of course, is that Paphos succumbed to the great disaster that felled Kourion, only twenty-five miles distant, in 365. As for Hilarion, English historian Robin Lane Fox tells us in his excellent new study, *Pagans and Christians*, that in the year 371, Hilarion died in Cyprus at the age of eighty, "to the usual Christian wrangle over his relics and the pieces of his body."

What does all this prove? Nothing certain, except that there were many observers and historians of the fourth century who testify to a great earthquake that most likely affected Sicily, Paphos, and Alexandria. Combined with the numismatic evidence, as we shall see presently, these accounts make a rather persuasive case that the great earthquake of July 21, 365, reported by Ammianus Marcellinus, was the disaster that brought down Kourion.

Thus we were beginning to pull together a comprehensive and plausible portrait of this disaster. The physical evidence was providing a cogent geological hypothesis, even fixing the epicenter of the temblor with a precision remarkable for an event sixteen centuries in the past. Still, as far as the archaeological community was concerned, it was nothing more than mildly interesting conjecture. Archaeologists are notoriously conservative and seldom willing to consider new ideas unless they are backed up with volumes of airtight proof. What we needed was to dig virgin territory and find a numismatic cache or some well-preserved pots—something—that would verify our hypothesis.

That would come later. Meanwhile, in the worldly scheme of managing and funding an excavation, things were beginning to go remarkably well. While our money problems had not exactly disappeared—like a socialite, an archaeologist can never be too rich—things had improved considerably over the first couple of summers. Missouri and Dartmouth had generously switched their funding from the digs at North Africa to those at Kourion, and Diana Buitron had brought in the support of the Walters Art Gallery in Baltimore. A small measure of recognition had been accorded us in the form of a commission for a story by *Archaeology*, the leading popular magazine in the field. Plans were well under way for rebuilding the temple of Apollo, based on everything we had discovered through excavation and archaeological detective work.

Most exciting of all was that the University of Missouri had put up the money for a half-hour documentary film about Kourion. It was to be no educational video but a real *movie*, with a real movie director, a man named David McAllister who had won prizes for his previous films, such as one about George Caleb Bingham, the nineteenth-century Missouri artist. Our film was to be called *Search for Apollo* (it came before Time-Life's blockbuster "Search for Alexander" exhibition and television series), and I was to write the script, design the story boards, and write and perform the music. (I had always had musical aspirations—when I was an undergraduate at Dartmouth I had played in a group called the Sphinx.)

"Our film": how exciting that phrase was for me! I had stepped through the silver screen and entered the fabulous realm of *The Journey to the Lost City*. I threw myself headlong into the film, all the while continuing to direct the excavation. It was great fun, and, though I did not realize it at the time, it was also tremendously draining. Just as the film was winding up its shooting schedule and as we were about to raise the front of the newly resurrected temple of Apollo, a nasty little bug known as the Coxsackie virus swept through Episkopi village, where we had set up our headquarters. Cyprus is infamous for its propensity for terrible local epidemics such as this one, which helps to explain why the villagers' folk religion is based so much on prayers to the Virgin Mary, St. Panteleimon, and other saints for intercession to preserve them against evil. Nonetheless, several children in Episkopi died, and many adults were very sick, including me.

In my exhausted state, I collapsed, racked by chills and a 106-degree fever. I was beset by hideous hallucinations: legions of yellow maggots surrounded me, covering my world whether I shut my eyes or opened them. And in the back of my mind lingered the thought, admittedly a bit ridiculous yet nonetheless awful, that perhaps I was the victim of a curse, the Curse of Kourion: that like George McFadden and J. F. Daniel, other interlopers in the realm of Apollo, I was going to die before my time. I knew this fear was an unreasonable fantasy of my feverish brain, the result of having watched too many B movies about vengeful mummies, but I could not shake it. When you are in a place in which superstition is still a powerful force, the familiar truths no longer seem so reassuring. Things that we usually snicker at can seem ominous when the comforts of civilization are stripped away. Some well-meaning soul placed a piece of the village's sacred tree, only recently cut down, by my bed.

After five days of raving, the fever broke. Perhaps coincidentally, the turning point came immediately after I asked that the piece of sacred wood be removed from my sickroom. Fortunately, the film had been more or less completed; a few scenes of my own, which I had saved for last, had to be done later, back in the States, using rear-screen projection and a sound track of crickets and tool sounds recorded in Cyprus.

Then, just as I was beginning to mend, I had a serious accident. Everyone had left Kourion except for a few of us, and Karageorghis was not satisfied that the site had been left in proper order. It was scarcely a week after my fever, yet I was stupidly trying to stack some wheelbarrows in a storage shed at the city site, and just as I was putting the last one on top, the whole pile fell on me, pinning me to the concrete floor. One of the barrows fell squarely on my left wrist and crushed it.

Karageorghis took the project of the temple reconstruction out of my hands while I recuperated and reassigned it to the renowned Greek restorer Stefanos Sinos, who had worked on, among other places, the Parthenon in Athens and the medieval religious complex at Mistra. Working with a generous grant from the government of Cyprus and with our full cooperation, Sinos set up a construction site behind the temple. Just like his ancient predecessor, the temple's original architect, he quarried stone from the earth nearby, cut it with painstaking care into columns, capitals, bases, and wall blocks, and hoisted it all into place. The reconstruction was completed in 1986. It had taken six years and come close to claiming the life of one of the excavators, and Sinos had changed some of our interpretations of what it looked like, but at last Cyprus had its first opportunity in nearly two thousand years to see what a Roman temple in the age of Nero might have looked like.

For the next three years, I cut back my work schedule considerably, as I slowly regained my strength. I continued to teach at the University of Missouri and to work in the field, albeit in a curtailed fashion. During this time, while working at Mirobriga, Portugal, I found what still seems to be the oldest Celtic temple known, directly underneath two later Romano-Celtic buildings. It was a remarkable discovery, but nobody cared, even in my own profession, where Portugal has always been given short shrift compared to Greece and the Near East.

My work at Kourion—and my ideas about the earthquake that destroyed it—had to wait until 1984. The young girl and her mule and her next-door neighbors, the young Christian family huddling together as their world collapsed, had waited sixteen centuries to be dug out of their stony graves, and they would have to wait three years more. It was a comparatively fallow period, a time for some reflection about what we were doing there, and indeed about the real meaning of the archaeologist's trade.

The "New" Archaeology

LIKE SO MANY THINGS with the sobriquet "new," the New Archaeology has been around for a while, fifteen years at least (though in the temporal context of classical archaeology, that is still new enough). It is only a phrase invented for the delectation of editors; nonetheless, it does mean something. There really has been a revolution of sorts in the way many of us are thinking about the field. In the past, in "classical" classical archaeology, the overriding concern was the discovery, or rather recovery, of beautiful objects from antiquity. Such blockbuster finds as those at Pompeii and Herculaneum, and particularly Howard Carter's spectacular hoard from the tomb of Tutankhamen, which he found in 1922, attuned archaeologists, and certainly the public, to the ideas that bigger was better and that gold was best of all. Nowadays, while archaeologists still have a healthy awareness of the value of gold and beautiful objects, our interest more and more is in what the unearthed object can tell us, to approach it from the socioeconomic as well as the aesthetic point of view. Of course, this approach in itself is not new—the glorious wall paintings at Pompeii, for instance, speak volumes about the life and thought of the gentry of imperial Rome. It is more a matter of motives —*why* does one dig?—and of what one does with the stuff after it comes out of the ground.

There are 6,528 Roman baths in the world, and we would all get along quite as well if another one were never found. To excavate per se is boring and pointless, if all you are going to do is dig up more objects to be tagged and catalogued and put in display cases with little white cards saying how old they are. Not that there is anything wrong with exhibits; certainly museum studies will always be an essential part of classical archaeology. But the more interesting questions for us now are, What did people *do* with this thing? Exactly what went on here?

These questions prompt others: Who would know? Who can help me answer the question? If I am a classical archaeologist, my training has been in Greek and Latin literature and linguistics, with some practical instruction in numismatics and the stylistic identification of pots and architectural decoration to the end of establishing a date and cultural sphere for a site. There is no reason why a classical archaeologist would have the slightest idea what to do with old bones, or charred vegetable remains in an oven, or animal droppings. Or, to cite another example, there I was excavating the site of an earthquake, and everything I knew about earthquakes, in the beginning, would have been barely enough for a passing mark in freshman geology. So, to answer these questions about the artifacts one finds —and the more curious one is, the better—one must recruit the people with the answers, the osteologists, botanists, and zoologists. The job of the archaeologist is to formulate the questions and to find the answers.

This may all sound quite obvious, and now that such practice has become widespread, it *is* obvious. Yet it was not very long ago that classical archaeologists were throwing away great quantities of artifacts simply because they were not up to museum exhibition standards or, worse, because they did not recognize them. The customary approach to a tomb site, for example, used to be to cull out all the jewelry and ceramics and anything else suitable for exhibition—and then to throw out the rest, including human remains! Archaeologists in Egypt used to grind up crocodile mummies to mulch their gardens. Nowadays, happily, archaeologists have turned to chemical fertilizers to enrich their gardens, and everyone in the field, except for a few curmudgeonly antiques, recognizes that the humblest scraps can tell us something, if only we are clever enough to entice that information out of them. As in business, diversification and recruitment of top talent are the keys.

In 1982, I left the University of Missouri for the Wild West: I became a professor and, soon, chairman of the department of classics at the University of Arizona in Tucson. Noelle and I missed our friends at Mizzou, but we took to the life in Arizona immediately: the majestic desert landscape, the unfailingly agreeable climate, and the cheery "can-do" western style were all very seductive. It was also an excellent place to practice archaeology; in fact, one of the pioneers of the New Archaeology, the dynamic Bill Dever, was working there.

Unlike many universities, where the divisions between departments can be somewhat ossified and inflexible, things at Arizona are wide open, and when I approached scientists to enlist their aid, they responded enthusiastically. There is an excellent reason for their interest, and it has to do with the current state of archaeology in the United States. In the past twenty years, the field has bifurcated into two almost entirely distinct disciplines: classical archaeology, which concentrates on sites in Europe and the Near East; and New World archaeology, which, as its name would suggest, focuses on the study of American Indian civilizations.

The differences in the two fields arose from the differences in the places and peoples they were studying. To state the most elementary truth imaginable, the ancient civilizations of the Mediterranean were quite literary and produced art of the highest quality; hence the necessity for classical archaeologists to be trained in Greek and Latin and art history. By contrast, the Indians of the New World (with the exception of the Maya) had no literature, and their best artworks, particularly in such highly impermanent media as textiles and feathers, tend to be fragile. In many cases New World archaeologists find themselves excavating sites that may consist of no more than the remains of a fire, some human droppings, and a few arrowheads, perhaps a pot or two if they are lucky. Working with such meager materials, they are forced to be clever at extracting as much information as possible from what artifacts they have. And to do so, they have turned to laboratory science.

This division between the two branches reveals what a bastard discipline archaeology is. The traditional divisions are breaking down throughout academia, but perhaps more than any other field, archaeology as it is currently being practiced is a hybrid between science and the humanities. The classical end of the field emphasizes the literary and aesthetic, and the New World branch emphasizes the scientific—but at a place like Arizona, we are all learning from one another. The European and Near Eastern archaeologists, especially the prehistorians, have sometimes been in the same boat as the New Worlders and used their ideas.

One of the most appealing aspects of digging at Kourion is the fact that, because it is the site of an earthquake, everything is still in its place; we can be reasonably sure that everything we find "belongs." That is one of the most vexatious questions that routinely present themselves to an archaeologist, and it is perhaps best explained by an example. Let us say that we have found a golden earring in an imperial-era private house. We do not know whether it belonged to the people who built the house, to a vandal who looted the place a hundred years later and squatted there, or to a tourist of the fairly recent past, who may have bought it in an antique shop and dropped it there accidentally. Nor do we know why there is just one of them: Was it a custom of these people to wear just one earring? Was the mate stolen? Did the original owner lose it on a trip to her mother-in-law's house for Sunday dinner?

Thus an archaeologist must continually hedge and qualify and "perhaps" everything he finds, for unless he happens to find some dated written record, he must always be skeptical about the provenance of anything he excavates; if he is not, his colleagues will assuredly be skeptical for him. Yet—and it is a big yet—at Kourion *everything* belongs. The site is a moment in time frozen and preserved, like a snapshot. If the Kourians had had clocks and wristwatches, we would know the exact hour and minute of the quake. That is important, for it clarifies the picture wonderfully and enables us in some cases to draw conclusions when ordinarily we must apologetically sketch in possibilities. There are a couple of minor exceptions: we found intermingled among some human remains the bones of a rodent, which we believe burrowed there after the quake to feed on the corpses. Yet that sort of thing in no way invalidates the rule.

The trend in academic studies nowadays is toward increasingly rarefied specialties and subspecialties; so there is a name for this one, too. We call it seismic archaeology, a subset, if you will, of the New Archaeology. Of course, all that term means is that we are studying ancient earthquakes; the point of it is exactly the same as ordinary archaeology except, as we have seen, without the headache of establishing provenance. Of course, the number of excavations doing seismic archaeology is limited by the number of earthquake-affected sites known. The field really began with Sir Arthur Evans, who observed the effects of seismic disasters in his famous excavation of the Minoan Palace at Knossos at the turn of the century. Evans used these seismic observations to stratify the cultural occupations of the site and to help establish his chronology of the ancient Cretan civilization.

Modern theorists in the field, such as George R. Rapp, Jr., at the University of Minnesota, are now pointing out that one must be cautious in jumping to seismic conclusions: there are many geological events (mud slides, for example) that can mimic the effects of an earthquake. For this reason, archaeologists must rely on the expertise of trained geoscientists in their work, or they may stray into errors. There are several important recent seismic digs in the Mediterranean: at a quake-ravaged temple at Petra, in Jordan, conducted by archaeologist Philip C. Hammond and his team from the University of Utah, and at a ruined Greek sanctuary in Cyrene, in eastern Libya, excavated by a group from Penn led by Donald White.

At Arizona, I began to think about another season at Kourion. My ideas about dating the quake there had been received by the archaeological community with skepticism and even ridicule. When I originally presented my theory to a conference in Nicosia, I was almost laughed off the podium. It did not help much when I tripped and fell on the dais.

Of course, such setbacks only whetted my desire to take down my spade and get back to work. I knew I was right; all I needed was a little excavational luck. Vassos Karageorghis, who continued to be supportive (though reserving judgment about my theories), gutsily invited me to come back to test them out. And the University of Arizona had promised, as one of the enticements for me to join the faculty, to support the excavation generously. Then I began my systematic pursuit of scientists in other departments at the university, recruiting paleoosteologists, zooarchaeologists, paleoethnobotanists (the sesquipedalian pileups can leave one breathless), a microstratigrapher to reconstruct the buildings, and more earth scientists to replot the quake itself. Of course, I could not know in advance whether all these people would have something to do when we arrived at Kourion; that would depend on what we found. Yet that summer of 1984, on our return campaign, it turned out that we were every one of us, as Walker Percy says, "busy as one-armed paperhangers."

Renewing the Offensive

LIKE A TEXAS WILDCATTER, we needed to find a good place to dig. Our license to return to Kourion was granted to us by Karageorghis specifically for the purpose of testing my hypotheses about the quake that had destroyed the city, especially my ideas about dating it. In fact our circumstances were exactly like a wildcatter's, for we did not have the time or the money for a "dry hole"; if we came away from this season with nothing, it would be very difficult indeed to go back to Karageorghis to ask for a permit for another year, or, what was more to the point, to raise money. In archaeology, as in any field, nothing succeeds like success. You are only as good as your last trench, and people wait with appalling glee to destroy your career through gossip. After one has made one's name, one is much more of a target: make a single mistake, and all of of your successes cease to exist.

To tell us where to dig, in place of a wildcatter geologist's report, we had the rather disorganized field diaries and photographs of the Penn expeditions in the 1930s and McFadden's brief, sporadic publications in *The Illustrated London News* and the *University of Pennsylvania Museum Bulletin*. We found many tantalizing tidbits, but the difficulty was in translating the various crumbs of data into an X on the spot where we could plant our spade. As we pored over them, one passage kept jumping out at me, this paragraph from one of McFadden's contributions to the Penn museum bulletin: "Both of the settlements which we have found, Greek and Roman, met with sudden catastrophes due to earthquakes. . . . In one of the rooms of a house which was part of the second floor, preserved in the walls, we found two skeletons, of a man and a woman, entangled in such a way as to suggest a Romeo and Juliet tragedy. On the girl's finger was a bronze and quite a lovely gold ring."

In another piece for the Penn museum bulletin, published in October 1940, McFadden, who for unknown reasons had changed his mind, described the same skeletons as two women "caught in the earthquake that brought down the house." The skeletons have been lost, but it later became clear, from the drawings and photographs we found, that there never was any Romeo and Juliet death embrace. Only one skeleton was intact, an adult lying on his side in the fetal position, both arms bent across the chest and the hands placed over the face for protection. The skull was facing toward the west, approximately the direction from which the earthquake emanated. A second adult skeleton was indeed present, but it survived only in part. Again oriented in a westerly direction, of this specimen only the legs and feet were recovered. As the skeletons were not correctly, or at least not completely, identified when first unearthed, it is

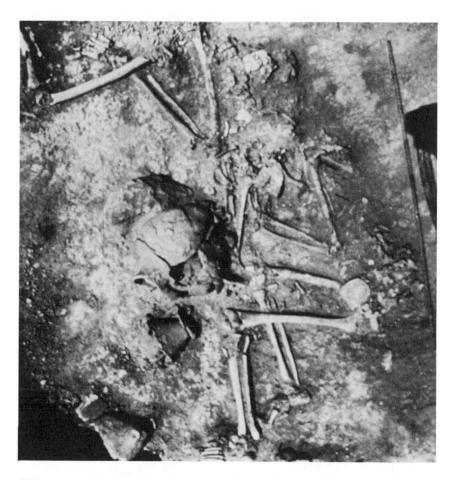

Fifty-year-old photographs such as this one are our only record of these skeletons, excavated in 1934 by J. F. Daniel, who gave them the fanciful nickname "Romeo and Juliet." At right is a full skeleton; at upper left, the legs of another. In the center of the photograph is a shattered storage jar, and just below it a copper alloy pitcher. The remains themselves are now lost. (COURTESY OF ROGER EDWARDS, UNIVERSITY OF PENNSYLVANIA)

possible that the rest of the second skeleton was shoveled away by the laborers in 1943 before anyone realized it was happening.

While McFadden did not fully understand the significance of the human remains—not at all unusual for an archaeologist of his era—he did make this astute observation: "That none returned to retrieve or bury the dead testifies to the magnitude and extent of the earthquake, and explains the catastrophe that overcame the Sanctuary of Apollo at the same time."

It sounded like the perfect place to test our theories about the earthquake: everything we knew about what McFadden and Daniel had found there in 1934, particularly the photographs of the skeletons, suggested that the area had not been disturbed by grave robbers in the period immediately following the earthquake. We were reasonably sure that no one had disturbed the area since the 1930s, for it had been under official control ever since then, and, as we have seen, no one had shown interest in digging there in the intervening fifty years. An intact postquake site was just what we needed, but Daniel in his diary had neglected to mention one critical point: where this house and trench were located. All we knew was that it was somewhere on the seaside edge of Kourion City. Without more specific information, we might be digging for years before we found it.

A trip to the Penn museum yielded the clue that the trench in which "Romeo and Juliet" had been found was called trench III by the McFadden expedition. Then Roger Edwards found a photograph of the two skeletons from the 1934 dig that had never been published. The accompanying portions of J. F. Daniel's field diary bolstered our conviction that trench III, if we could locate it, was the place for us to dig: in addition to everything else, it was in the debris here that, according to the diary, he had found coins from the reign of Valens, the em-

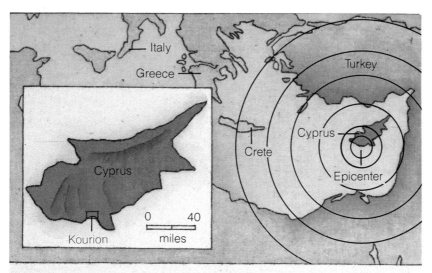

Italy

Greece

Turkey

Cyprus

Crete

Cyprus

Epicenter

Kourion

0   40
miles

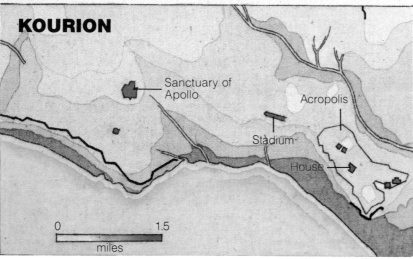

KOURION

Sanctuary of
Apollo

Acropolis

Stadium

House

0   1.5
miles

(Ron Becker)

Kourion at dusk. Members of the dig raise a camera to the top of the Whittlesey Bipod. At lower right is room two, where the remains of Camelia and her mule were discovered. (*Janelle Weakley*)

1986. This view of the house is from the west, with rooms six and seven in the foreground. The foundation of the central column in room eight (center of photograph) was torqued by the earthquake. (*Noelle Soren*)

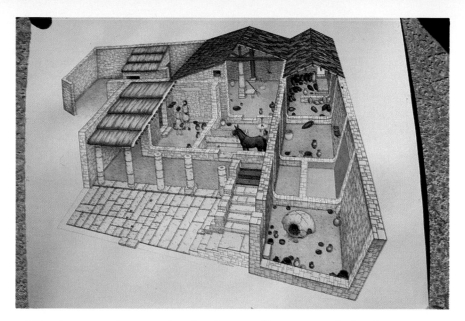

The layout of rooms in the house. Room two is in the center, room one is to the left, and room eight is at the rear. In the foreground is room sixteen; the steps on its right side originally led up to a rooftop platform surrounding a cistern, room twelve (the blank area at right). In the right foreground is room fourteen, the kitchen. (*David Vandenberg*)

Kourion on the eve of the great earthquake of A.D. 365. The house is at rear, and the imposing edifice at right is the Market. The animals shown here are all represented in the faunal remains from the site. (*David Vandenberg, courtesy National Geographic Society.*)

This painting shows how room eight might have looked just before the final earthquake of A.D. 365. (*David Vandenberg*)

An artist's imaginative view of the same rooms just before the earthquake. The man and woman examining the pot are J. F. Daniel's "Romeo and Juliet." (*Jim Bryant*/Discover *Magazine* © *1987, Discover Publications Inc.*)

This photograph of rooms one, two, and three was taken with a camera on the Whittlesey Bipod. The mule's skeleton lies next to the trough, skewed by the earthquake. (*John Huffstot*)

Room two in 1984, with the mule's skeleton still where we found it, tethered to the eight-hundred-pound stone feeding trough. (*John Huffstot*)

In 1986 we found these skeletons, almost certainly the remains of a young Christian family. A computer drawing untangles the skeletons: the man in violet, the woman in orange, the baby in red. The scattered position of the baby's bones is the result of scavenging rodents after the earthquake. (*Photographs: Martha Cooper, courtesy National Geographic Society; drawing: John Sanders and Peggy Sanders*)

Walter Birkby, the forensic anthropologist on the dig, here delicately cleans away debris from the fallen plaster molding that broke the young woman's neck. (*Ines Vaz Pinto*)

Room six must have been a storeroom of some kind. (*Janelle Weakley*)

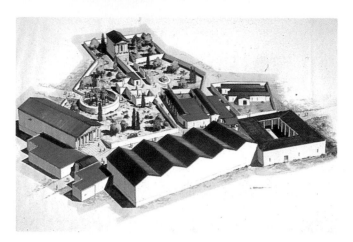

The sanctuary of Apollo at Kourion as it might have appeared in its heyday, in the second century of the Christian era. The temple of Apollo is at the rear. The paved street, which served as the worshipers' principal access, runs diagonally down to the antebuildings, in the foreground. To the left of the street is the round building, in the middle of a small park. Directly across the street from the park is the archaic altar. (*Jim Bryant/* Discover *Magazine* © *1987, Discover Publications Inc.*)

This aerial photograph shows the sanctuary of Apollo as it is today. The tin roofs at right cover the sanctuary baths. (*Helicopter 84 Sqn. R.A.F./*Discover *Magazine* © *1987, Discover Publications Inc.*)

peror who had ascended the throne in 364. It was very, very promising, but we still had to find the damn place.

Then, in a nice bit of luck, I came across a plan of the city that had been drawn by Joseph Last, McFadden's architect. The original had been lost, but epigrapher Terrence Mitford had published it in his book *The Inscriptions of Kourion.* In that plan, greatly reduced and difficult to read, was a trench identical in outline to the sketch of trench III in Daniel's field diary; furthermore, it was labeled with a barely visible "III." We had our X at last. So all of us, with all our various specialties, descended on Kourion, hopeful that this tissue of logical inference would hold up in the cold (or in this case searingly hot) light of day. John Huffstot, our architect that season, was assigned the task of matching the X on Last's plan with an X on the actual site. In my schedule for the season, I allotted two weeks to find it. Huffstot left for the site early the first day. Within ten minutes, before I could finish breakfast and bring over our second carload of diggers, he was standing over the site, his head characteristically bobbing up and down, as he uttered the phrase that was to become our battle cry that summer on Cyprus: "No problem."

On the fiftieth anniversary, as it happened, of the digging of trench III, we began to excavate in the same spot, on a high bluff overlooking the Mediterranean, just a few meters from the theater. It is a fine example of an imperial Roman theater, which was fully restored in 1961 by the Cyprus Department of Antiquities and is once again in operation, catering to the English military personnel stationed nearby and the considerable summer tourist industry. In an ironical twist too hokey even for Fritz Lang, on the day we discovered the stony tomb of McFadden's star-crossed lovers, the Kourion theater was offering a production of Shakespeare's *Romeo and Juliet.*

83

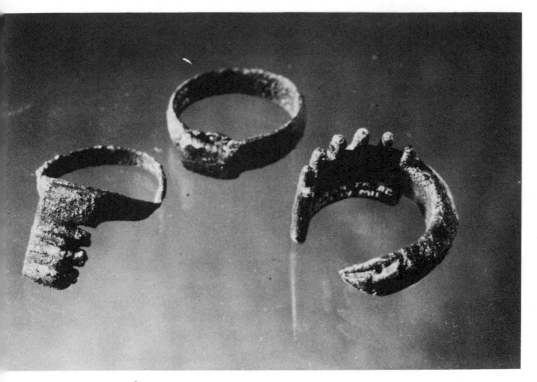

*Three rings from a jewelry collection in room one. The one at the right
is in the form of a snake; the one at the left was used as a key.* (MARTHA
COOPER, COURTESY NATIONAL GEOGRAPHIC SOCIETY)

As we dug our way into Daniel's trench III, which we re-
named room one, we found no more evidence of Romeo and
Juliet, save one tooth, one toe, and a phalanx bone. We did find
some interesting jewelry, including a copper ring carved to
look like a tiny coiled serpent; and two pretty deep-sea conchs;
Romeo, no doubt, was a good diver and brought them up as
gifts for Juliet. We also found something much more to the
point: in islands of collapsed earthquake debris, which had
been left undisturbed by McFadden's workmen, we found

thirty-eight copper asses. (The as was a Roman coin that at this time was worth a few cents.) And while some were a bit earlier, many of them were characteristic of early issues from the reign of Valens, from the years 364 and 365!

We know almost as much about the coins issued in the Roman Empire as we do about the currencies of modern states. The Romans were nothing if not efficient record-keepers, and they were especially scrupulous about keeping track of their money. Roman issues did not bear dates the way a modern American coin does. There was also a great deal of variety in Roman coins, and the different mints operated independently of one another, so there sometimes exists a certain amount of ambiguity. Nonetheless, we can usually be quite specific in the matter of dating.

The first coins issued in the reign of Valens—at least from the mint of Constantinople, about which we have the most information during this period—are distinguishable by the fact that the emperor's name is broken. That is, on the obverse ("heads") side, where appears the bas relief of the emperor's head in profile, the letters VALEN appear to the left of the head, and the final s is at the right. The Roman minters must have decided that breaking the emperor's name was not the height of style, so sometime before September 28, 365, at least in Constantinople, they introduced a new design, which did not break the imperial name. While we do not have the same certainty about other mints that we have about the one at Constantinople (information, it ought to be pointed out, that comes from modern scholars, not from our own coin hoard excavated at Kourion), it is nonetheless reasonable to assume that they conformed generally to the practices there. In any case, the broken-s form of "Valens" is believed to be characteristic of the early part of his reign.

85

Now, of the forty coins we have unearthed at Kourion that bear Valens's name, thirty-three are of the split-name type, and only seven have the name unsplit. According to the report of our numismatist Eugene Lane, "If the destruction had taken place later in the period . . . one would have expected the reverse ratio." In other words, the unsplit mintage had just recently come into circulation, strongly supporting a mid-365 date for the earthquake. Continues Lane, "Now, it is known that the change in legend must have taken place before 28 September 365, [the date of the] usurpation of Procopius. . . . Thus a date in mid-365 seems dictated by the numismatic evidence *alone*." Another important deduction may be drawn from the hoard, in this case not from what is in it but from what is not: there are no coins dating to the reign of the usurper Procopius, which reinforces what was generally supposed, that he never exercised any control over Cyprus. Even more telling, there are also no coins of Gratian, who became co-emperor in 367.

Of course, there are many old coins in our hoard (including one from the reign of Claudius more than three hundred years before, which might have belonged to a classical coin collector). Eighteen coins came from Antioch, a city that had close communications with Cyprus. Also well represented were the mint at Cyzicus, in western Asia Minor, with eight, and that at Alexandria, with five. Three coins came from Nicomedia; Heraclea and Thessalonike each contributed two; and mints represented by a single coin were Aquileia, Sisak in Yugoslavia, Constantinople, and Rome. We have only one coin that might undo our tissue of logical suppositions, a piece that, writes Lane, "may be at least 37 years after the destruction, which would have to have crept in from subsequent re-occupation, but which is too effaced to identify with any certainty."

86

These finds are certainly going to make it difficult for anyone who wishes to argue for the previously held, earlier earthquake dates. Now those people must explain how coins minted from late 364 through September 365 found their way into virgin earthquake debris. In 1985, we found thirty-four more coins. They were mostly in bad condition, but they followed the pattern of the 1984 hoard and thus tended to support our interpretation.

After our success in room one, we decided to expand. We moved to the next room to the northwest, which had never been excavated. We called it—what else?—room two, in the great archaeological tradition of drearily prosaic names. After removing the meter or so of sandy soil, we hit the jackpot, in the form of virgin collapse. Here we found twenty-four coins and fragments of the glass vessel that may have held them. The range of dates in these coins was the same as among those we had unearthed in room one. Pressing on to room three, along the same northwest axis, we found more evidence of the temblor's power. At least half a dozen pots had exploded in the quake and scattered all over the room. A threshold weighing more than a hundred pounds had been ripped loose from the ground and rotated ninety degrees from its original position.

Several meters below the surface, the earthen floor of the room appeared. Here we discovered a silver-plated bone hairpin, a well-preserved spatula, an olive pit—and more copper coins, this time 113 of them. As before, the coins all fitted the pattern that my theory of the earthquake's date had predicted: a few were of earlier date, but several were early issues of the reign of Valens, and nothing had to be dated after 365. By this time we were feeling quite confident, if not altogether vindicated. It was only thirty days into the campaign, and we had already proved our point. Now we were ready for even bigger game, and we found it, right under our noses in room two: our first human victim of the disaster.

Room two was the only space that we were able to excavate completely in that first return season, and we soon deduced that it was not a room at all but a hastily improvised stable. Originally, rooms one and two had been one larger space, but a crudely built cross wall had been inserted and the animal feeding trough introduced. This hypothesis was verified when we found the remains of a mule, still tethered by an iron chain to a stone feeding trough. This trough provided us with the most graphic testimony yet to the awesome power of this quake. Weighing more than eight hundred pounds, the trough had been lifted up by the shock wave and hurled against the southeast wall of the stable, denting the wall. A pulse also snapped the trough in two like a candy cane. The hind legs of the mule had given out under it as the ground turned to Jell-O beneath its feet, disorienting and terrifying the animal. And next to the mule's hindquarters, we found the remains of a young girl.

As we slowly and carefully extracted the child's bones from the earth, the picture of her last moments of life began to take shape. We all shared a deep sense of intimacy with her as we lifted her remains from the ground. If our conclusions are right, it had been very early in the morning, before dawn, when the temblor occurred. Camelia (our name for the girl) must have woken up when she heard the mule whinnying anxiously, for it is well known to seismologists, folklorists, and zoologists alike that animals are sensitive to seismic upheavals long before humans notice anything. She went out to calm the beast, who was perhaps her workmate. Then the disaster struck. The earth trembled sickeningly, the glass jar of coins fell from the shelf with a crash, the half-roof of the stable collapsed. As her world came crashing down over her, as she was

The muzzle of the mule found in room two, partly excavated. Visible at right is the bronze ring for the bridle by which the mule was tethered to the stone trough, still in place. (NOELLE SOREN)

buried alive in stone, her hairpin, perhaps a gift from her mother ("Juliet," in the adjoining room, wore one identical to it), came flying out of her hair. The last sounds she heard were the hysterical neighing of her mule and the screams of "Romeo and Juliet," who might well have been her parents, inside the house.

Next, our multifarious scientific team moved into place to do its work. Our forensic anthropologists, Walter Birkby and Alison Galloway, reconstructed the girl's shattered skeleton. They determined that when Camelia fell, she was turning her head toward the southwest—the direction from which the shock wave and most of the flying debris were coming. She probably died very quickly from severe trauma. After the first wave she was most likely still alive and crawling through the rubble. When the second wave hit about four seconds later, she fell face down, her hands covering her face. Most of her bones must have been broken and crushed in the shower of stone.

We had all supposed that she was a girl by the presence of the hairpin, but because of differences in size and formation between men's and women's teeth, Birkby and Galloway were able to sex the skeleton beyond any doubt through a comparative analysis. A dental study also made her age approximately thirteen; but after the forensic anthropologists measured her bones, they found them to be quite small, the size of a modern eleven-year-old's. Proceeding logically, Galloway and Birkby at first inferred that the girl's diminutive stature had resulted from the fact that she was crippled. However, as more bodies have come to light, it has become apparent that ancient Cypriots were simply quite small people, many less than five feet tall, and they now think that Camelia was in relatively good health.

Her teeth, at least, were in good shape, which suggests that her diet was a fairly coarse one; Camelia, like most Greek peo-

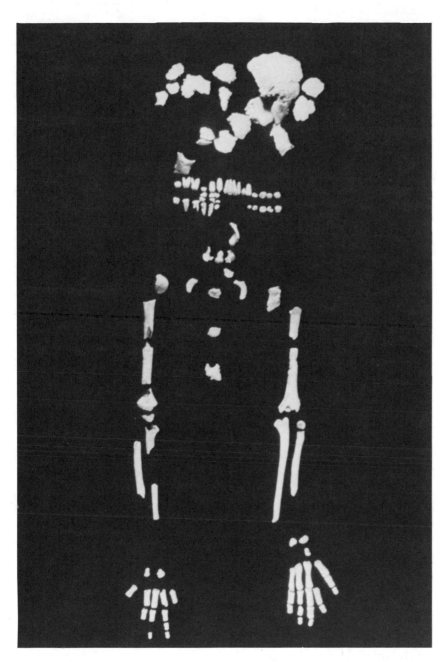

The crushed remains of the thirteen-year-old girl we call Camelia. (JA-NELLE WEAKLEY)

ples of this era, had no cavities. In the recent spectacular archaeological discoveries at the seaside edge of Herculaneum, dozens and dozens of human victims were studied by paleoosteologist Sarah Bizell. She observed the same extremely fine degree of dental health and attributes it at least in part to the relative lack of sugar in the diet. Another factor contributing to the soundness of ancient teeth is the fact that their owners got more jaw exercise from chewing because food tended not to be cut up into little pieces. (There were no forks until the seventeenth century.)

The one abnormality that did turn up was a remarkable thickening of the victims' parietal bones, the back plates of the skull. That may be the result of iron-deficient anemia, which could have been caused by an episode of malaria, a disease that has afflicted Cypriots since the Stone Age; alternatively, it may have been caused nutritionally. A trace-element analysis carried out by atomic spectrophotometry at the Analytical Laboratory of the University of Arizona showed a high level of arsenic. The elder Pliny tells us, however, that that poisonous element, used as a liniment, was a favorite Roman cure for coughs and sore throats.

The reason that most of these conclusions must be so heavily larded with "mights" and "maybes" is that, until we began to unearth some of Camelia's neighbors, Galloway and Birkby had virtually nothing with which to compare her remains. The essence of forensic work is comparative analysis, setting an unidentified bone side by side with one of which the whole story is well known. Only by a comparison of the chemical analysis of one corpse with the findings for a large population can a forensic scientist say whether a certain substance exists overabundantly or is deficient.

One of the valuable contributions that the Kourion dig may

ultimately make is to provide anthropologists for the first time with a reliable and complete cross section of an ancient Mediterranean city. Any skewing of the specimen population will undermine the accuracy of the identification in a particular case, as happened to our own excellent forensic anthropologists, who were temporarily thrown off by Camelia's small size compared with modern girls her age but perhaps not with other Cypriot girls of the latter fourth century.

With the exception of Herculaneum, human skeletal analyses in the ancient Mediterranean have had to be based primarily on burial populations, which are not especially accurate because they contain an excessively high proportion of babies and elderly people. Because everyone in this district of Kourion was trapped at the same moment, the excavation offers an unprecedented opportunity for compiling the first trustworthy sample of a classical society in situ. The victims of Vesuvius at Herculaneum had such a long warning time that many people were able to escape and thus were not found in their usual habitats. (No complete skeletons were recovered at Pompeii. There, decayed human remains left molds in the volcanic ash, which could then be filled with plaster.) At Kourion, however, death came without warning, burying the fleet and the halt side by side, which means that after we have unearthed more we shall have a representative census of this estimable city. Further, we shall be able to break it down by age, sex, health, and even in some cases by religious affiliation.

In terms of artistic finds, Kourion has not yet yielded a great trove of museum-ready artifacts. Nonetheless, we have come up with a number of quite nice items, and among the most pleasing are some copper-alloy lamps. While copper lamps can be helpful in the cause of dating, they can also be deceptive: because they did not break and were often of great artistic value, they were frequently kept as heirlooms, just as fine jewelry will generally be passed down in a family while costume jewelry perhaps will not. Nonetheless, copper lamps are of considerable artistic interest, representing a much higher level of artisanship than their clay counterparts. Lamps of this era came in any number of different forms, but the basic function of all was the same: a wick floating in a bowl of oil will burn where it surfaces, and a fist-sized lamp could burn for an entire dinner party. The oil could be extracted from sesame seeds, nuts, or fish, but olive oil was the principal fuel employed throughout the Mediterranean. Wicks could be made from linen, papyrus, flax, and possibly even asbestos, oddly enough.

Here in Camelia's stable, we found an elegantly wrought copper-alloy volute lamp (one having a spout that is bordered with spiral decorations), with a separately manufactured finial in the shape of a leaf. It was found near the surface, at the beginning of our excavation, just below the southeastern wall of the room, which made it difficult to fix its location in the room. The experts who have examined it say it is in the Italian style and date it to the first century of the Christian era, which would have made it a three-hundred-year-old heirloom to its owner at the time of the quake—the equivalent of a Louis XIV chair to us. A lamp specialist from the University of Delaware named Steven Sidebotham has found analogues in two clay lamps from Carthage, both dated to the first century. When our team conservator cleaned this lamp, some well-preserved wicks were found in the interior. Examination by scanning-electron microscopy at the Metropolitan Museum of Art in New York City showed them to be made of bast fiber, probably flax, which is what the elder Pliny is talking about in his *Natural History* when he writes: "[The part of the flax] nearest the skin is called oakum. It is flax of inferior quality, and mostly . . . fit for lamp wicks." We were all very buoyed up by this discovery. It is rare indeed to find organic matter in a state of preservation that permits such a precise identification.

Another copper lamp, one that genuinely surprised us, was

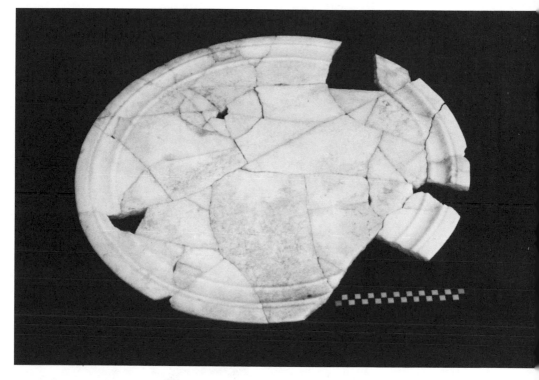

This marble tabletop, also from room two, first smashed down the middle and then fragmented further. The marble comes from the Greek islands. (JANELLE WEAKLEY)

found in the stable, quite an elaborate cast lampstand with attached lamp, which had sat on a marble tabletop. The tabletop had been shattered into pieces, which were found scattered all around the room, though the majority of them formed a kind of ring around the lampstand. The table fragments were helpful

95

This spiral-shafted copper-alloy standing lamp, of the Hellenistic period, was recovered in room two. The hat-style lamp was supported by a tripod of dolphin-headed figures. The shaft may have been bent by the earthquake. (JOHN HUFFSTOT)

in demonstrating the severity of the quake here, suggesting that objects were hurtling around explosively in every direction. Standing copper lamps and marble tables are most inappropriately fancy furnishings for a stable, the sole usual inhabitant of which presumably was the mule—rather like having a Persian rug and a horsehair divan in the garage. The lampstand has a tripod base, with curved legs ending in stylized representations of human feet. Above the feet is a thin disc that curves upward, like a stylized image of a flower. From this base rises a spiral stem in the form of a Corinthian column and capital, out of which spring three dolphin heads, which support a small lamp. The lamp was badly damaged but was found still attached to its stand. The lampstand was bent, apparently during the earthquake or perhaps later during the aftershocks and the settling of debris, though there is no reason why it might not have bent while it was still in use.

This type of lampstand-lamp combination is by no means unheard of, but we have not yet been able to locate another quite like it. Its closest relative also comes from Kourion. It was found in the forum area by the Cypriot archaeologist Demos Christou. It also has a floral tab above the tripod base, but the stem is plain except for a single vine winding round it, intermittently hung with bunches of grapes. Footed candelabra of fine quality occur in Etruria from the first century B.C. There is one quite similar to ours from Boscoreale, near Pompeii, which has pediform legs (in the shape of lion paws) and a floral tab above it—but the stem is more delicate. Significantly, while spiral shafts are quite common among the Etruscans, the Romans seem not to have fancied them. Pompeiians chose fluted shafts for their lampstands.

The lamp itself is an open or hat lamp, a very primitive type consisting simply of a dish pinched at three corners (whence its name, as it resembles a tricorne hat). The dish is filled with oil, and the pinched corners hold the wicks. Hat lamps were common in the Near East from the Early Bronze Age and seem to have undergone a revival in the late Hellenistic period, but, at least in clay, they were no longer manufactured after the second century B.C. That seems like an attractive date for our lamp, one which the style of the Corinthian capital also supports. Thus it might have been an Etruscan import from about this time, or it might have been a local Cypriot knock-off in the Etruscan manner. In any case, it is a very strange item to find in a stable—of which more anon.

As the 1984 season wound down, we plunged ahead and began excavating a new room, adjoining room two on the northwest axis. In room three, as we called it, we unearthed a wide variety of things: several large storage jars, a fineware plate (which had probably been imported rather recently from southwestern Asia Minor), a grayish cup, a pithos, a torpedo-shaped amphora, a spatula, and some bronze coins. There was only a solitary olive pit to tell us what the room's tenant used all that crockery for, not that it told us much: the presence of olives is always a safe bet in the Mediterranean. The key find here was a very well-preserved clay lamp. Unlike copper lamps, which tend to be unique, aesthetically significant objects, clay lamps were as common as fleas in ancient Cyprus and are now endlessly useful as index fossils, for identifying and dating purposes.

The phrase "index fossil" is borrowed from paleontology, and it is quite perfectly apt. Just as a paleontologist knows when he comes across the fossilized remains of a woolly mammoth that he is mining a stratum of the late Pleistocene era, so an archaeologist can be sure when he comes across a known lamp type exactly which culture and what era he is excavating. Or, another analogy, one might think of index fossils as the art direction of archaeology: when one sees a snapshot with a finned Cadillac and a woman wearing a pillbox hat, one can be reasonably sure that the photograph was taken in the early 1960s. Reasonably sure, but not positive: while the ancients did not share our passion for nostalgia, in the sense of reviving fossilized fashions—many trend-following ladies in the 1980s wear pillbox hats—nonetheless they venerated the past and were fond of keeping heirlooms. So, while one must maintain what amounts to an adversary relationship with everything one's spade turns up, index fossils like clay lamps are indispensable in knowing, literally, where you are.

This particular lamp from room three is an example of a lamp known as Vessberg type 18, so called after the German scholar who classified many varieties of lamps. Like all Vessberg 18s, it has an oval body and a short nozzle. The shoulder is decorated with a relief that depicts bunches of grapes and a sinuous branching grapevine. The concave upper surface, which is called the discus, is decorated with the image of a man striding to the right. A semicircle delineates his hair, while eyes, nose, and nipples are indistinct blobs. He appears to be wearing a loincloth consisting of one strip around the waist and vertical strips hanging down over the genitals. At the figure's feet is an amphora. With his left arm, he points to an inscription that reads ITE ALIS, while his right arm holds an enigmatic, crosshatched object that has been variously described as a vase, a basket, or a fish.

One intriguing interpretation of this object is that it is early Christian in its iconography. Most lamps of this type, in place of ALIS, read ALIEI, which is the dative form of *alieus*, meaning "man of the sea"; thus the dative means something along the

99

lines of "for the fisherman." Accordingly, the object in the figure's hand becomes a fish, which, as we have seen, was an early symbol for Christ, and the figure would be Christ himself, "the fisher of men." Another interpretation has the figure not as Christ but as an early martyr of the Christian community in Cyprus, for the image of Christ holding a fish, a symbol of himself, is not a conventional early Christian icon.

This is an ingenious reading of the piece, and it is certainly a tempting one, as it so neatly supports our hypothesis that Kourion was by this time a Christian city. In archaeology as in any scholarly field, however, one must beware of letting the wish be the father to the thought. It is sometimes difficult not to find what one hopes will be there, but one must try to be as suspicious as one can of nifty explanations that fit one's theory perfectly. The hitch here is that the same inscription occurs on a lamp with no "fisherman" at all but rather a horse at full gallop. One of our colleagues suggested that the horse, too, was a Christian symbol, but that seems to be pushing it.

Another view takes the literal meaning of ALIEI, "sea man," and applies it to Poseidon, who is more easily identified with horses, certainly, than is Christ. Yet another view is that the inscription, translated straightforwardly as "for the fisherman," and the loinclothed figure holding the fish may refer to the lamp's owner. In other words, it may have been a lamp issued expressly for the use of fishermen, in the same way that a modern lamp for a seaside cottage or a boat will have nautical motifs in its designs.

However, the lamp in question says ITE ALIS, not ALIEI. One must always consider the possibility that a variation in word forms may be due to local slang usage or an analphabetic potter, just as misspelled words and fractured English are to be found on many modern products and in their instruction booklets. Yet ITE ALIS may be translated as "Go ye forth in abundance," a felicitous phrase that accords perfectly well both with a fisherman and with a gamboling horse. Such a cheerful thought, exactly the sort of thing beloved by Greeks and Romans, would be quite appropriate and welcome at banquets or for use in everyday life.

This last seems to be the best interpretation for the lamp. If all this seems very unsettled and indistinct, that's because it is. More often than not, one cannot finally say, This is definitely what this object is, and we can be quite sure that it was used for such-and-such a purpose. The only people who know the answers to all our questions are the people who died in the earthquake. In this case, we must content ourselves with outlining all the possible and reasonable explanations of the data, but, as in a mystery novel with the ending ripped out, we shall never know which hypothesis is the correct one, unless some new and unanticipated piece of evidence should come along to settle the matter for us once and for all. Barring that eventuality, the most we can do is simply endorse the most plausible explanation.

As the 1984 season drew to a close, I found that the question that kept revolving in my mind was the riddle of the marble table and the Etruscan-derived (or whatever it is) copper lamp-stand in the stable. What was it doing there, along with two other copper-alloy lamps? It was certainly a luxurious accommodation that Camelia and her family kept for their mule. At that point I first began to think that they were poor people who had appropriated this once-elegant establishment, now down at the heels. Perhaps one of the earlier earthquakes had ruined the house, and after its original inhabitants, who may have been the family of a rich trader or planter, abandoned it, these lamp-collecting folk took over the place. That story would explain the impromptu atmosphere of the household. The bronzes, thus, might not be heirlooms but rather objects left behind by the original tenants.

Of course, I was not yet thinking of them as Christians—for the reasons already stated, I was not at all persuaded that the fisherman lamp was Christian, and at that point we had not found the ring inscribed with the chi rho. It was just an idea simmering on the back burner of my mind.

The 1985 Season

AFTER THE SPLASH of publicity we received when we discovered the remains of Camelia and her mule, it was a bit easier to get people to look at our work. In 1985 we were able to corral backing from the National Geographic Society and the National Endowment for the Humanities. We were also supported by the Hellenic Cultural Foundation, an ad hoc group of distinguished Greek Tucsonans who got together to raise money for us. It was our grandest dig yet, in terms of personnel and the area excavated. We were finally able to get a sense of the extent of the house. Now that we were concentrating on the topographical and architectural aspects of the site, we began to use computers, which are revolutionizing archaeology just as they are every other field. And computing, as it happens, adapts very naturally to traditional excavating techniques.

Frank Brown, my mentor and longtime resident of the American Academy in Rome, once took me aside to tell me that archaeology may very profitably be regarded as the systematic destruction of a place. A site has been covered with dirt for hundreds or thousands of years; and it is perfectly content to remain buried. The archaeologist wants to know what is there, so he dismantles the whole area and carts away everything of interest—as well as much that may seem to be of very little interest—for further, more detailed study. Yet it must be emphasized that it is a *systematic* destruction, with the precise location of every item, and every observable condition of its discovery, carefully noted down. Otherwise, after the season is over, the whole area fades away into a confusion of indecipherable tags and conflicting recollections of what was found where.

The usual method of recording archaeological finds is to impose a conceptual three-dimensional grid on the site using ordinary surveying methods, and when something—anything—is found, the coordinates are recorded. Until recently, this procedure meant that you ended the summer with lots of dusty, sweat-stained notebooks and charts, all covered with numbers. You do not have to be a computing expert to see that data processing equipment is ideally suited to the organization and manipulation of records from an archaeological site.

The surveying techniques that we use at the field house in Kourion are more or less the same as those used by the original construction team that built the house: plumbs, strings, and line levels, plane tables and stadia rods. Instead of scribbling the numbers down in little pads while we were in the field, however, we used hand-held Hewlett Packard computers. Whenever anything was unearthed, our computing specialists,

John and Peggy Sanders, would enter a complete description and the coordinates of the find in computer language, thus eliminating the tedious (and error-introducing) task of having to reenter all the data into the excavation's computer back at camp. A further capability of our computer system is that it can convert all those numbers directly into graphic representations of the site. We are also able to record drawings of the site and the finds through the use of a "sketchpad" computer program, which allows one actually to draw on the computer and enter these two-dimensional figures into the machine's memory. Thus, at the end of each season, we have a complete compendium of every scrap of information pertaining to the dig, all broken down and cross-referenced in every imaginable way.

As the data are all fitted into the three-dimensional framework, it is possible for our computer whizzes, with a few deft key pulses (they do not call it button-pushing any more), to create a drawing of the site from any angle, in perfect perspective, with the various elements highlighted in different colors. Another few strokes, and the picture is transformed into a floor plan or an elevation, with or without representations of any combination of the finds. And any of these computer drawings may be copied quite easily. Needless to say, this technology has made life quite a lot easier for us. In the "old days" (that is to say before 1985, when we adopted this computer system), all of these drawings had to be done by hand, completely from scratch, requiring at least a full day to execute. Now we can crank them out as quickly as we think them up.

We continued to dig in the same northwesterly direction as before, but the next rooms we found, room four and room five, proved to be a bust; in fact, we now believe that they are part of another building altogether. At least this discovery showed us that the ruins extend beyond the first house. Yet so as to avoid

The view across room six, filled with restored pots, toward room eight, minutes after dawn. Work at the dig begins at first light. (MARTHA COOPER, COURTESY NATIONAL GEOGRAPHIC SOCIETY)

piecing together two houses at once, we backtracked to room three and turned west, which turned out to be an excellent move. The two rooms we found here, inevitably called rooms six and seven, formed the western corner of the house; in room six, we found the remains of a staircase, of which two steps and a rubble foundation survive, that led up to the street. They must have been storerooms, for they were jammed with things: amphorae, jars, cups, glass vessels, and a funnel, more than forty items altogether.

Amphorae often have good stories to tell. Clay vases—typically cylindrical, with a narrow neck and two handles, and usually fitting into a tripod—they were the most common vessels of antiquity. They often serve as index fossils, but they are unreliable because the same style was often made in the same place for centuries and centuries. Rather, amphorae help to fit a site into the ancient economy, showing the scholar what imports the city brought in and from where, from which one may extrapolate important political information. Amphorae are classified by shape, material, contents (which may be determined through chemical analysis in the laboratory), and any inscriptions they may bear. Many of the amphorae found at Kourion are of the "plump" body shape, which may have been locally produced. That they were of Cypriot manufacture we infer, in the first place, because they are so common. Furthermore, the mineral composition of the gritty, reddish-brown clay is quite similar to the petrology of the Troödos Massif, the mountainous region of central Cyprus that is the island's principal geological feature.

Another amphora from Kourion has a heavy, oblate shape known as the "bag-shaped" body. This distinctive amphora form is well known in the Near East for its association with Gaza, the ancient city in Palestine. A piece of this amphora was

This amphora from Gaza may have held white wine. (NOELLE SOREN)

This amphora, of a type not previously known, was the most common at Kourion and may have been of Cypriot manufacture. (JANELLE WEAKLEY)

sent to the University of Southampton (England), which has a center for the study of clays and ceramics from the ancient Mediterranean. David Williams, one of the principal scholars at Southampton, examined our shard under the microscope and found bits of white limestone, quartz, and even fossil remains, together with a few grains of pyroxene. As a rather striking example of the remarkable continuities in this part of the world, when he compared this ancient vessel with a modern clay vase from Gaza, he found that the composition was very similar. Williams has not yet determined what the vessel held, but based on its type and probable place of origin, it may have held *gazetum*, the white wine that Gaza exported throughout the Mediterranean.

Another common type has an ovoid body with a round base, broad neck, and thick stumpy handles. These amphorae often have painting known as *dipinto*, in a cursive red Greek script, on the pinkish-cream surfaces of their shoulders. These markings seem to be nothing more than notations of capacity. We believe that these vessels come from Antioch, in northern Syria, which had a booming export trade in olive oil. We subjected some shards from one of these amphorae to a sophisticated form of chemical analysis called high-performance liquid chromatography, which revealed residual traces of olive oil. This connection with Antioch is significant because that city was a major center of Christianity in the eastern Mediterranean.

At Kourion we attach far more importance than usual to the conservation of the things we find. We devote as much of our time and resources to this aspect of the dig as to any other, for we feel strongly that it is an integral part of the expedition. Thus we have five full-time conservators, while most digs have

Two conservationists mend amphorae in the field laboratory. (MARTHA
COOPER, COURTESY NATIONAL GEOGRAPHIC SOCIETY)

only one. Our overall emphasis at Kourion is on the reconstruction of ancient life, and there is a special pleasure in seeing
the articles of everyday life restored to a state close to their
original condition and returned to their actual positions at the
time of the earthquake. By the 1986 season we were already
thinking in terms of establishing a site museum at Kourion,
and for that purpose we needed to restore as many objects as
possible.

The conservators' task was a difficult one, owing to some
problems peculiar to the site. The climate on the south coast of

Cyprus is subject to great extremes, from nippy winters to withering summer heat, from foggy damps to drought. Also, the earthquake itself created enormous problems. Whereas at most digs one finds scattered shards—or sometimes, in tombs, whole pots—here the clay and glass were smashed to smithereens by falling stone and mortar during the quake. Thus the job of reconstituting these vessels has been tremendously difficult, especially when many pots of similar clay fabric were standing together, as in rooms six and seven. It was as though the beads of a dozen almost identical necklaces were dumped into a box together. Our conservation team, led by Terry Weisser of the Walters Art Gallery, Jane Carpenter of the Brooklyn Museum, and Marian Kaminitz of the American Museum of Natural History in New York City, was able to expedite this work a bit through the use of the dig's computer system, which was able to remember all the different shapes and locations of shattered shards far better than the people who entered them into its memory with the sketchpad program designed especially for our use. Nonetheless, it was still mostly a laborious process of trial and error. As the shards were gathered from the site, all of the pieces from a particular area were grouped together and given a basket number. Of course, pieces of some pots overlapped into different baskets, but it helped us to keep track of what was found where.

Once all the pieces of a pot were found and matched, the conservators glued them back together again. They brought with them various sophisticated adhesives specifically designed for museum use. When their supplies ran out, they had to go to the local supermarket in Limassol and buy tubes of a humble glue called Bostik—the same over-the-counter preparation Cypriot housewives use to mend broken teacups. Afterward,

Three extremely rare pottery forms recovered at Kourion: (left to right) a fineware vessel (which may have been a pitcher reused as a bowl after it was broken in antiquity), a two-handled cup, and a pilgrim flask. (NOELLE SOREN)

the pots were repositioned, according to their basket numbers, in their original places, and photographed.

The metal objects, particularly the coin hoard, presented a special problem, for they were so badly corroded as to be completely illegible. That created something of a dilemma, indeed almost a power struggle. I needed the coins cleaned as soon as possible for purposes of dating and identification; but the conservators, as is their wont, lobbied for the safest and slowest methods. The reader will perhaps not be surprised to learn that the dig director won out, particularly since the coins were hardly art treasures and were in very bad shape.

The method finally settled on for cleaning the coins was a highly ingenious electrolytic process that is far safer than the stripping solutions, usually acid, that were commonly used in the past. It is simple, really: the bronze coin is placed in an electrolytic solution and connected to a more noble metal, in this case a stainless steel spoon, creating thereby an elementary, extremely weak electric battery, the bronze coin being the cathode, the spoon the anode. The resulting electrolysis gently removes all the corrosion, allowing one to reach the stable metal beneath (unless, as was often the case, the corrosion was so bad that the coin had been eaten smooth).

The glass objects were seriously weakened by prolonged exposure to the Cypriot soil. Their component sodium and potassium ions had leached out of the glass and into the soil, stripping away layers of the silica. This process creates the iridescent optical effect so common in excavated glassware. When the ancients used them, these objects were transparent and plain, like modern glass; yet this leaching process has created the impression among countless museumgoers that opalescent stemware was all the rage in classical days. At Kourion the alkaline soil damaged the glass so badly that in some cases little more than a few shimmery flakes remained. Where more of the glass survived, the conservators were able to hold the silica layers together with resin.

Running alongside rooms six and seven and flanked on its end by the stable where Camelia and her mule perished, was a very large, open room. It had in the center a single column, consisting of two limestone drums superposed on a base of limestone slabs. The doorway giving access to Camelia's stable had been blocked up, lending credence to the idea that the house had been subdivided by several tenants at the time of the quake. The roof beams, hewn of cypress and pine, had become infested with borers, perhaps termites, which had deposited their excrement in the surviving bits of wood. Nevertheless, Michael Schiffer, our formation processes expert, ascertained that this room had all of its roof tiles. He was able to determine that from the apparently hopeless heap of rubble by counting up all the corner pieces and dividing by four, which thus gave him the total number of tiles. This fact is important, first because it shows that the ceiling had not collapsed earlier, and second because it tends to support the hypothesis that this part of the house was not robbed. Room eight was the only one in the house to have a full complement of tiles.

The furnishings had a harum-scarum, miscellaneous feel. Here we found a copper-alloy lamp similar to the one in Camelia's stable, except that this one was fitted for hanging. Three little chains, attached to holes on both sides and on the finial, join above the lamp and suspend it from a larger chain, which in turn depends from a delicate hook. These chains, which were unearthed with the lamp, had been damaged and repaired in antiquity. The discus is decorated with a bas relief of a wreath prettily tied up with ribbons at the top. It was ingeniously fashioned to accommodate seven wicks at a time, which allowed it to burn very brightly. Nearby, in the northern corner of the room, were two quite lovely copper-alloy pitchers, to which had been added feet. An alabaster table, with only fragments of its original feet, had been propped up crudely near the central column. The table had been badly broken by the house's collapse in the earthquake. We also found three complete pots, an iron axhead with traces of its wooden handle,

These bronze proportional dividers, a common draftsman's tool used to reduce and enlarge designs, were found in room eight. (JANELLE WEAKLEY)

two grinding stones, an iron knife, the jawbone of a cat, and, curiously, an intact pair of artist's proportional dividers wrought of copper alloy. What had seemed to be the remains of a pitchfork could not be identified with certainty.

Think of this as an English drawing-room murder mystery: how can one account for all of these things being immured together? The correct answer, of course, is that we can never be entirely certain. In archaeology as in life, the world is intractably accidental and idiosyncratic. Yet we are nonetheless able to draw several reasonable hypotheses about room eight: the many tools lead one to suppose that it was most likely used as a miscellaneous workroom. Yet it might also have been someone's homestead; our hypothetical residents at the time of the big earthquake did not divide the rooms of the house according to function the way the original tenants, presumably a single family and their servants, had.

It is hard to find good architectural parallels for this house. Significantly, it does not seem to follow the pattern either of the Italian atrium-centered house or of the later Greek house models. The closest parallels are with contemporary Cypriot village architecture: the use of mud bricks and stone chinking, reinforced with rough ashlars; threshold blocks elevated above the courtyard; central column supports, such as that in room eight; and the general standard of living all more closely resemble a modern farmhouse in the nearby village of Kato Kivides than anything known from classical times in the Mediterranean. The second-phase usage of the building (namely, at the time of the earthquake) also has a modern analogue in the architecture of the village of Paramali, where the houses commonly situate the sleeping quarters alongside the stables to help keep them warm.

In room eight, we made great headway with the analysis of the actual effects of the earthquake. Here, geologists found some evidence that the quake that destroyed Kourion actually comprised three separate shocks. They are properly called waves, and for once the jargon provides us with a helpful image of the process at work. The first, called the primary wave, brought down the roof tiles, sliding them down into the room as the central column buckled, as well as toppling the higher mud bricks of the walls. Seismologist Terry C. Wallace now estimates, based upon the approximate epicenter and the geological character of the region, that this phase lasted four seconds, and had a ground acceleration of .1 g, where 1 g is equal to the normal force of gravity. While this pulse would have caused severe disorientation, the people and animals could have survived it. Camelia and the mule, for example, had significant amounts of rubble *underneath* them, and they were probably struggling up through the debris when the second pulse hit.

The secondary, or shear, wave was the killer. It lasted ten seconds with a g force of .35, representing rapid, regular oscillations. Wallace assigns that force a .7 disorientation factor—something really hellish, in Wallace's phrase "like being underwater in the dark and not knowing which way is up." He gives the quake overall a 7.25 on the Richter scale. Because of the close control we kept over the microstratigraphical deposits—in other words, by observing the actual rubble and dirt—it was possible to hypothesize that the shear wave followed the primary wave by three to five seconds.

The tertiary wave, which came immediately after the second, lasted five seconds. In this shock, the rapidity of oscillation and thus disorientation decreased gradually. The tertiary wave, according to Reuben Bullard, was more sinuous in its motion, realigning walls and floors in a wavy pattern, especially at the stable, where it cracked through the trough. Wallace, however, is not convinced by this model of the tertiary wave's effects. It ought to be stated here that not every piece fell to the northeast, though there was a general tendency in that direction in the second wave. Some things simply collapsed. Part of the southeast wall of room eight, for example, just gave way. In an earthquake of this type, not everything falls in a uniform way, as there are other factors involved. One seeks rather to establish the overall trend.

One reasonable hypothesis about room eight is that it was once a reception room, or perhaps the *triclinium* (dining room) of this elegant house. Then, after an earthquake earlier in the fourth century—we have several to choose from, the most likely of which were in 332 or 342—it was so badly damaged that it was abandoned as a grand hall. Then less prosperous inhabitants moved into the house and began to divide it up. Room eight, one might suppose, belonged to someone of limited means who turned the place into a workroom; and while he was not terribly prosperous, he nonetheless kept a cat as a pet and drew pictures for a hobby. Now, the question was, where was he?

The grisly answer to this question awaited us in the next room we opened in the house, an even larger room (later named eleven-b) situated southeast of room eight. Here we found the skeletal remains of a man in his fifties who had taken refuge in a doorway and was then crushed to death by falling stone ashlars. The concussion was so traumatic that his teeth flew out of his mouth; his torso was wedged between hundred-pound limestone blocks. The strangest and most gruesome aspect of this find was that his entire lower body was missing. The corpse would have been situated rather high up in the postquake debris, unprotected by any masonry, which led Walt Birkby to suppose that his lower body was torn away and eaten by animals, perhaps wild dogs looking for food after the quake. The bones that did survive were in better condition than most of the ones we have found, enabling the physical anthropologists to determine that the man, first of all, was a man, that he was a robust, well-built fellow, probably a manual laborer, and that he was suffering from osteoarthritis in his back.

Room eleven (rooms nine and ten, like four and five—if they are rooms at all, rather than streets, alleys, or courtyards—lie

outside the house proper) was by far the biggest we have yet
found; in fact, as it continued to stretch on and on, for conve-
nience we divided it into sections a, b, c, and d. The latter two,
we realized after a while, were actually an adjoining courtyard;
but no matter, for these designations are completely arbitrary.
One could just as easily name the different rooms at a site after
one's favorite movie stars or ice cream flavors.

In the southwestern corner of the room we found hundreds
of fragments of a plaster wall painting, still in situ. The pieces
we were able to recover, all in terrible condition, belonged to a
decorative frieze that included the figure of a bearded man or
god, foliage, and inscriptions in Greek, perhaps identifying the
figures. Exactly what the painting depicted we shall never
know, but the conventional thing would have been a mythological incident or an epic cycle, such as an episode from the Trojan War or the wanderings of Odysseus. The mural seems to
have fallen in an earlier temblor and then to have been compacted to a new surface, which was in turn destroyed by the
big earthquake. In other words, the painting never had much
of a chance to survive. We analyzed some of the fragments in
the laboratory under polarized light microscopy and found evidence of both types of plaster mural painting prevalent at this
time: they are, to call them by the names given them by artists
of the Italian Renaissance, the *buon fresco* technique, the applica-
tion of wet paints onto wet plaster; and *fresco secco,* which uses
plaster itself as the medium and a dry plaster ground.

The artist used a rather large and sophisticated palette by
fourth-century standards, including yellow ocher, Egyptian
blue, ground hematite for the red hues, and calcined bone
(bone reduced into powder by heat) for both the black and the
dark blue colors, a rather unusual practice in Roman times.
These fragments are tantalizing; it is like having a handful of

pieces from a gigantic jigsaw puzzle, not even enough to guess what the picture might have been. Perhaps another painting in better condition will be found elsewhere in the neighborhood. Also, fragments of mosaic are turning up, scattered about the surface soil north of the current excavations.

Here we also found more pieces of logical support (if not quite evidence) for the thesis that the house had been appropriated and subdivided by settlers at the time of the quake, in the form of impromptu adaptations of architectural materials. In the doorway that connected rooms eight and eleven, the ancient dwellers had crudely reused a capital from an anta (a sort of pilaster, normally placed at the entry to the interior of a temple) as the doorstep between the two rooms. Even more intriguing, the floor of room eleven seems to have been covered in rubble *before* the final quake; and the threshold block on the room's northeast side (between rooms eleven-c and eighteen) had a hole cut in it, apparently for tethering animals. That fact raises the possibility that this salon-sized room, containing an elegant fresco, was by the time of the quake exposed to the elements and filled with rubble and had mules or asses abiding in it.

Furthermore, in the northern corner of room eleven we also found a small area that had been cleared of rubble in ancient times, apparently after the final quake. It contained patches of lightly compacted sandy earth and traces of small fires. It is quite possible that this place was a temporary campsite for some survivor or survivors of the earthquake. Incidentally, this is the only place in Kourion we have found thus far that might have been a locus of postquake squatting, although the fires may have been lit before the quake and just not covered with fallen rubble. In the soil layer here we also found a coin from the reign of Valens.

In the corner, in room eleven-a, we found quite a large clay oven, of the simple hemispherical type common throughout all antiquity in all parts of the Mediterranean world. This room could well have been a communal kitchen for the immediate area. There was certainly every evidence that it was in use at the time of the earthquake.

At the conclusion of the 1985 season, Linda Pierce, a zooarchaeologist at the University of Arizona, prepared a report on all the faunal remains found at the city site. Most of them were garbage from food preparation, including sheep, cattle, goats, and pigs, as well as numerous chickens. It is difficult to apply positively our postulate that everything found at a seismic site such as Kourion must "belong," must have been there at the time of the disaster. For example, the rodent whose bones were found intermingled with Camelia's remains most likely crawled down through the rubble after the quake to feed on the girl's corpse, then got trapped there itself in a further subsidence. Likewise, the cat in room eight, which we hypothesized earlier to have been the pet of the human tenants, could just as easily have been a wild postquake scavenger. We have also identified the remains of some small game birds such as quail or partridges, and what may be a snake.

The 1986 Season

WHILE THE 1985 SEASON was a thoroughly gratifying success, in 1986 we streamlined the staff and became more of a lean, mean archaeological machine. Everyone who came with us in 1985 was excellent at what they did, but the size of the group made effective communications difficult. A slightly smaller expedition proved more efficient.

Yet even with fewer people plying spades (though we added some help from local village labor), in 1986 we uncovered the greatest area yet in Kourion City. First, we dug some probes in the area west of the house, to see what lay around it. We found a street there, which we were able to date to the latter first to early second centuries of the Christian era. The walls of an earlier building had stood here, but it appears that when the Kourians built the street and our house, this building was covered over.

Nevertheless, we took a pass for the moment on this chance to learn more about early Kourion and shifted our attention to the opposite (northern) end of the house, near where we had begun. Northeast of room three, and catty-corner to the stable where Camelia died, we found a cistern in a rather peculiar space. We called it room twelve, though it is not a room in the ordinary sense, for it had no apparent means of ingress. The only way to get to it was from the second-story landing, whence, presumably, one could have lowered a bucket into the water. The walls of the cistern went right up to the second story. The tank occupied only half of room twelve. The rest of the space, conventionally, would have been given over to food storage. The great tank of water would have been cool in the summer and might have helped to preserve perishables, making it exactly a classical refrigerator.

Originally, at least, this water reservoir was well thought out and carefully maintained. One of my graduate students, a physics whiz, calculated mathematically that the tank was strong enough to withstand the pressure of the hundreds of gallons of water it would have held when full. The inner walls were lined with high-quality waterproof plaster. In one layer, we excavated a deposit of the sort of fine silty material that accumulates in water tanks. Here we found a beautiful necklace, a particularly affecting find. Obviously, it had fallen off a woman's neck while she was drawing water, and either she did not realize where she had lost it or she decided to leave it at the bottom of the cistern and forgot it when the normal cleaning time rolled around. So it was left to us to find it for her. The necklace had sixty-nine beads: sixty-three of pink coral, five of amber, and one jet bead. The coral most likely came from the Gulf of 'Aqaba, which is still the main source for this material. The

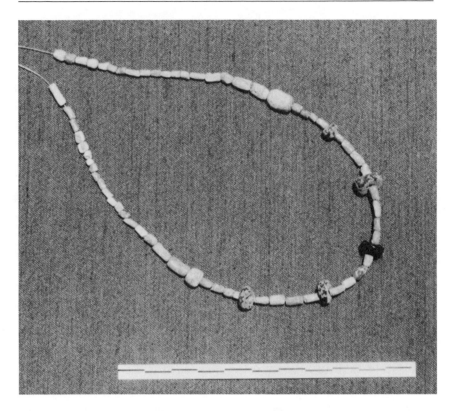

In the cistern of room twelve, we found this necklace composed of small beads of coral, larger beads of amber, and one of jet. The original arrangement of the beads is not known. (NOELLE SOREN)

amber may have come from Jordan, while the jet ornament might have come from Asia Minor, where such stones were known in antiquity as *gagates*, after the town of Gagai. The string, of course, had long since deteriorated, so it is impossible to do more than suggest the necklace's design. The cistern also yielded a broken silver-plated copper-alloy bracelet.

By the time of the earthquake, the cistern was most likely no longer used to keep potable water—either that or the ancient

Kourians had rather casual hygienic standards by our lights. We also found here some fish bones, charcoal and fine ash, broken pots, and the ubiquitous olive pit. The interpretation that best fits the facts is that the water reservoir belonged to the building's vanished grander days, and when the house became a dwelling for more transient tenants, it lapsed into use as a garbage dump.

By microscopically examining soil samples from the cistern and elsewhere, we were able to gain additional insights into the Kourian diet. We brought some soil samples back with us to Tucson, where paleobotanist Karen Adams studied them. First, she poured small quantities of the dirt into water, and the material that floated was skimmed off the top and examined under a powerful microscope. We have to discount a great deal of what is thereby collected—insect and rodent parts and feces, roots, twigs, and land snails—as modern intrusions into the earthquake stratum. By contrast, anything that was burned we may safely take to be contemporary with the earthquake. And in this category we found seeds of the fat hen (a succulent plant with edible leaves and seeds), Italian cypress seeds, woody cone scales, and something very like the seed of a fig tree. All of which proves nothing, of course; yet one might very reasonably suppose that an ancient Kourian of modest means made a fire of cypress wood and cones for the purpose of cooking a dinner that included fat hen.

Adjoining the cistern (though not communicating with it) was a kitchen, room fourteen, the northernmost room of the house. It was dominated by a large oven, which was smashed to bits by the earthquake. It was the same type of oven as the one we found in room eleven, the simple clay hemisphere still in use in Cypriot villages today. It was constructed of mud brick more than two centimeters thick and was about twenty centimeters high and wide. In the modern era, these ovens are usually located outdoors, for the compelling reason that it would be fantastically hot to keep a fire going indoors during the Cypriot summer. However, there exists no evidence that this kitchen was roofed; possibly it was a walled-in precinct, open to the air, which would allow the smoke and cooking fumes to escape.

Here we also discovered seven pots, including, in the corner, an intact pithos, a common type of large earthenware storage jar. A hole had been cut into it on the side facing into the room, and next to it was a stone that appeared to have been fitted for use as a bung, which indicates that the pithos had served as a permanent storage receptacle. We also found here all the other appurtenances of a kitchen, including three cooking pots; a handsome bronze pitcher; an orange bowl, the handle of which had a thumb-impressed decoration, a common enough phenomenon; and remains of three amphorae, including a complete one of the Gaza type. The fragments of perhaps twenty lamps were here, too, suggesting that cooking was sometimes a nocturnal activity. There were also six copper coins, including one that was probably from the early reign of Valens, and a single bronze fishhook.

Completing this commissary complex is a little pantry next to the cistern room, underneath the stairway that led up to the second-story landing above the water tank. This space we dignified with the designation room nineteen, though it is tiny, scarcely three meters long and a bit over a meter wide. Access was obtained from the courtyard that lay to the west of the kitchen-cistern area. The threshold was worn quite smooth, indicating that whatever went on in this place went on often. We did not find anything to speak of here—tiny fragments of

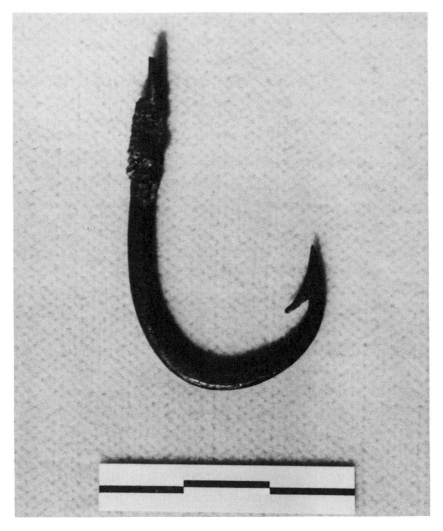

Bronze fishhook found in room fourteen, the kitchen, alongside some fish bones. (NOELLE SOREN)

animal bones, glass, contemporary pottery shards, one bronze coin worn smooth, and a couple of nails—which leads one to suspect that the closet might have been a storage room for something that would have vanished without a trace, such as fodder for the mule. Alternatively, it may have been a cupboard that happened at the time of the quake to be, like the one of proverb, bare.

This closet came at the end of a courtyard with a colonnaded portico that ran along its western side. This portico apparently sheltered those who entered the house and passed through the courtyard, and fronted the stable where Camelia and the mule died; then it ran south and turned a corner, wrapping around room one—"Romeo and Juliet's" chamber—which was originally excavated by J. F. Daniel and the Penn expedition in 1934. We called the southernmost, recessed part of the porch room eighteen and the colonnaded portico room fifteen, but they run into each other without interruption as a continuous space.

The colonnade had fallen sometime *before* the earthquake of 365 and was then crudely and partly rebuilt: we have recovered twelve fragments of broken columns and five well-made Doric capitals that had originally constituted it. We also excavated an earthen floor, which, significantly, lay above the level of the original floor in this area. And in the eastern corner of the paved court several column shafts and a capital had been stacked, and on top of them a crude basin installed, with mortared walls resting on the pavement. The basin might have replaced the cistern as a coolant for perishable foods.

These discoveries are crucial, because they show that the original portico had come down before the great quake of A.D. 365. An amphora handle found in the mortar of the basin was identical to dozens that had still been in use at the time of the big quake. The wall between the porch and room one showed signs of crude patching. All of this impromptu rebuilding and column-drum stacking supports the thesis that after an earlier quake had rendered the house no longer suitable as a grand residence, a second wave of settlers broke the dwelling up into smaller efficiency apartments with a sharply reduced standard of living. We also found two more simple ovens in the courtyard, ordinarily not a sign of prosperity and order in a dwelling.

One of our team of archaeological geologists, Frank Koucky, estimates that the earlier quake might have measured an eight (out of twelve) on the Modified Mercalli Scale, as opposed to the eleven of the 365 temblor. The date of the prior earthquake cannot be fixed precisely, but according to Koucky it was probably not too much earlier than the big one. We know from several ancient reporters that Salamis, on the eastern coast, was hit with heavy quakes in 332 and 342. One of them might also have shaken up Kourion, inflicting serious damage (like bringing down the colonnade around the courtyard) and leaving the house shabby, perhaps even squalid, but not uninhabitable.

On the eastern side of the paved courtyard we found two more rooms, which might have been the original entrance to the house. Room twenty, which occupied the better part of this side of the patio, resembles a propylon, or arched gateway, and room twenty-five (our numbering scheme having by now lapsed into a hither-and-yon yet nonetheless serviceable chaos), at its side, could have been a guardroom, servant's quarters, or storage room. The evidence seems to point in the direction of the two rooms having been converted after the first earthquake, or at least sometime prior to the quake of 365 into yet another self-contained living space. Thus, the main entrance to the house would have been shifted from here to room eighteen, the recessed part of the porch around the Camelia complex, which would have meant that the portico was not as necessary as before.

We discovered this circular cult building—in Greek, *tholos*—in 1978. The mysterious pits are just discernible in the upper part of the circle. (*Harry Heywood*)

We found this bronze ring in 1986 by the skeleton of the young man. The inscribed characters chi *(X)* and rho *(P)* form the beginning of the word "Christ"; in Latin characters they also suggest *pax*, "peace." (*Martha Cooper, courtesy National Geographic Society*)

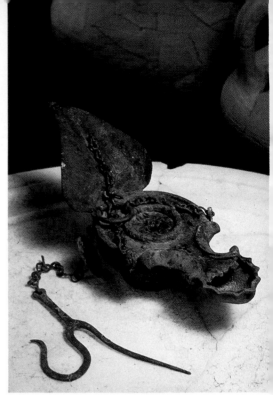

1987. This lamp is one of the most important Roman bronzes ever excavated on Cyprus. The hinged pour hole for replenishing the fuel supply still functions. (*Noelle Soren*)

This bronze hanging lamp, which was discovered in room eight, is shown here on the marble table from room two. (*Martha Cooper, courtesy National Geographic Society*)

Coins provide the most important clues for dating the earthquake that leveled Kourion. Altogether, we have excavated more than four hundred Roman coins. The coin pictured here is of the split-S variety. (*Martha Cooper, courtesy National Geographic Society*)

This engraved marble represents the head of a lion, which may be attacking another beast. It was found in the unsorted dump from J. F. Daniel's 1934 excavation. (*Noelle Soren*)

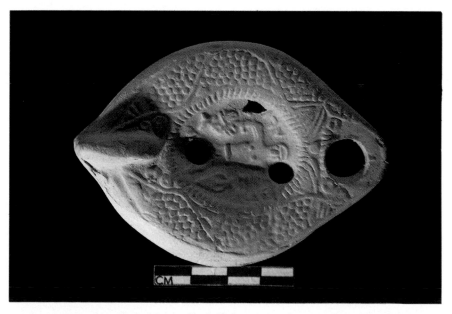

An example of the so-called fisherman lamp. (*Janelle Weakley*)

This bronze pitcher was in room fourteen. Six bronze pitchers have so far been unearthed at Kourion. (*Noelle Soren*)

A pedimental block, also from the facade of the market, believed to date from the late first or early second century of the Christian era. (*Noelle Soren*)

A molded cornice block, seen from below, still retains some of its original paint. This piece comes from the facade of the market building excavated in 1987. (*Noelle Soren*)

Room thirty. In the foreground, an earthquake victim clutched his head as the world came tumbling down. At the rear of the room, the outer wall of the building tips forward perilously. (*Martha Cooper, courtesy National Geographic Society*)

In this mosaic panel from a house on the western edge of Kourion, two gladiators—Margareites and Hellenikos—square off for a confrontation. (*Noelle Soren*)

This mosaic is from the floor of a house called the House of the Achilles Mosaic. It shows Odysseus, at right, unmasking Achilles, who is disguised as a woman. (*Jamie James*)

A group of Corinthian capitals recovered from the forum at Kourion. (*Jamie James*)

The mosaic of ΚΤΙϹΙϹ is from the *frigidarium* of the baths in the house of Eustolios. (*Jamie James*)

A mosaic pavement from the house of Eustolios. (*Noelle Soren*)

The basilica at Kourion was built in the fifth century of the
Christian era, utilizing materials from several pagan buildings.
Its construction was probably supervised by Bishop Zeno who
represented the Church of Cyprus at the Third Ecumenical
Council at Ephesus in A.D. 431. (*Jamie James*)

The partly reconstructed temple of Apollo at the sanctuary of
Apollo in Kourion. (*Jamie James*)

We were not able to finish excavating these rooms in the 1986 season, but what we found was of exceptional interest and high quality. In room twenty-five we came up with two amphorae, a unique red slip bowl with elaborate stamped decoration, and a copper knife. Yet the major discovery awaited us in room twenty.

There, on the very last day of the excavation as we were preparing to head back to the States, we unearthed the Christian family. McFadden had his Romeo and Juliet, at least for a while, but here was something even more moving, a young man and woman and a baby. The female, according to Walt Birkby, was about nineteen years old, with a height of four feet eight and one-half inches. Her neck had been broken and snapped to a right angle by falling rock debris, a large chunk of mortar and several rocks had entered her skull. Three arched blocks of stone, originally part of a decorative facade (perhaps belonging to the hypothetical gateway), had fallen on her. These fragments were in a remarkable state of preservation, still bearing traces of the original purple, yellow, and red paint.

In her arms she held an eighteen-month-old baby to her breast and face; when we found the child, its skull was still cradled in her bent arms, and its right hand was grasping the mother's left elbow joint. The child's legs were bent, the right leg resting on mother's right leg. Next to and behind the woman was the skeleton of the man. At five feet three inches, he was a bit larger, though the two of them support the idea that the ancient Cypriots were a diminutive race. His crushed skull was pressed against her shoulder near the area where her neck had been broken; and his spine was crushed by falling rocks.

We shall never know if this was indeed a young married

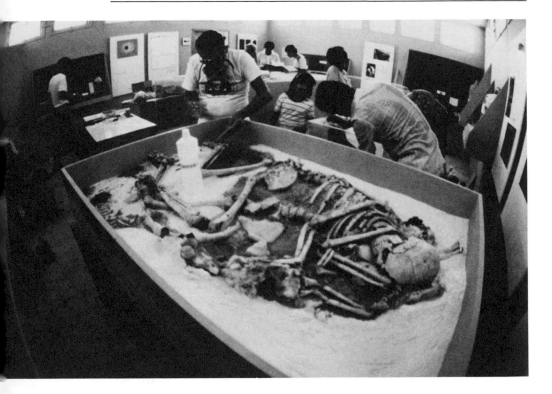

Forensic anthropologist Walter Birkby prepares the exhibit of the young Christian family for the new museum at Kourion. (MARTHA COOPER, COURTESY NATIONAL GEOGRAPHIC SOCIETY)

couple and their baby. It is possible that they are not; indeed it falls within the realm of the theoretically possible that they are all complete strangers. Yet the presumption that they are a family is supported by the circumstantial evidence. The man was clearly attempting to shield the woman and the baby at the time of their deaths. His left arm was covering her breast, while his left hand enfolded the baby's lower back. His right leg was drawn up over the legs and pelvis of the woman. As we removed the earth from them clod by clod, we could plainly see that the adult skeletons were pressed close to each other, with the male in the protective position. Both of them struggled to shield the baby, surely *their* baby, as enormous blocks, cobbles, and mortar exploded above and finally entombed them. There was also evidence of rodent action. The soft flesh of the adults' hands and the child's entire body had been disturbed.

And then we found the bronze ring inscribed with the chi rho and the alpha and omega. There were two rings, actually, just above the man's hands. (The other one, plain, was wrought of iron.) In every dig, out of the tons of pottery and bones and ancient garbage, and above all dirt, there is always one object that stands out as the most important, the most telling. There are famous cases, like the golden mask of Mycenae that prompted Heinrich Schliemann, when he found it, to cable the King of Greece, "I have gazed upon the face of Agamemnon!" (Of course, the mask antedates a historical Agamemnon by several centuries.) Yet more often, the pièce de résistance, the key to the puzzle, is something humble. At Kourion, it was that bronze ring incised with the simple symbol denoting the name of Christ.

This ring, in the moment we unearthed it, told us more than the thousand spadefuls that came before: it gave us the context, the theme, the motif of everything else at the site. Of course, we "understood" what we were excavating before we found the ring, but our understanding existed in a vacuum, or at least in thin air. While a coin or a thigh bone belonging to a Christian in no way differs from a pagan thigh bone or coin, it nonetheless changes everything to know which condition obtains. Although we know, comparatively, a great deal about the daily life of pagans in this part of the Mediterranean, the Christian world remains more elusive. Although the empire had become officially Christian, as chronicled in the opening chapters of

133

this book, in the hinterlands like Cyprus (in other words, in most places that constituted the empire), the Christians themselves were still by and large poor people, like the settlers who appropriated this earthquake-ruined house, and while they left a formidable legacy of literature, archaeologically speaking they were a fugitive race.

Now, at last, we have the chance to study the life of an early Christian community in this part of the world. And it is exactly its fugitiveness, its lack of "civilization" in the sense that an archaeologist ordinarily uses the word, that interests us. We know from the literature and above all from history how viable and strong was their civilization; yet it would seem that they took Christ at his word when he said that his kingdom was not of this world. What one may discern in the spare remains of these early Cypriot Christians is a hardy people who must have been sustained by a rich spiritual life, for their temporal life, it seems, was hard indeed.

The Summer of 1987

THE ARCHAEOLOGISTS' TRADE requires a certain amount of brazen and fearless predicting. Ordinarily, it need not be quite up to the level of Nostradamus; no one expects you to know all the answers. But one must at least, like Johnny Carson's Karnak, know what the right questions are. And nothing is quite as gratifying as to have events justify one's prognostications, when subsequent excavations turn up support for a theory or a hunch—which is what happened in the summer of 1987. Many discoveries in this season provided quite specific corroboration for some of our suppositions about the events at Kourion in the fourth century—including startling support for the Christian identity of the settlement. In some cases this corroboration is simply a matter of duplication: a singly occurring instance of anything, whether a style of temple or pot, a seed or animal bone, might prove to be an anomaly. But when another example turns up, it more than doubles the chances that a genuine insight into the excavated community has been made.

That is particularly true when it applies to people. Animals and plants and geological formations tend to be regular about obeying the laws that govern them. Man, on the other hand, is notably idiosyncratic, and his idiosyncrasies, furthermore, explain most anomalies: if a strange kind of plant or rock occurs, it is often because man, in every age the collector, has brought it there. In other words, one must be very cautious about making assertions about the human population on a dig.

To outsiders, archaeologists' glee upon discovering a human body often seems a bit sinister, smacking of necrophilia. Yet it is true, to coin a rather ghoulish formula, that for an archaeologist one corpse is worth a thousand pots. There is the obvious and very Greek explanation that, man being the measure of all things, the remains of a person offer the most important information. Because we are usually excavating a human place—a house or a palace or a campfire—finding out about the people who lived in a particular location is the most vital information we can uncover.

At the same time, perhaps archaeologists are simply ghoulish. Whatever the reason, an almost audible thrill of excitement rippled across the site when we hit our first skeleton of the 1987 season. This earthquake victim, a man in his early twenties who was pulverized by a shower of heavy roof tiles, was the first of three discoveries of human remains at Kourion that year. We now feel reasonably confident, as confident as we are ever going to be, in saying that there were few if any survivors of this quake. Anywhere a body was likely to have been found, one has been found. An estimate of the death toll of this earthquake, considering the number of bodies found thus far and the extent of the city yet to be excavated, would be somewhere in the neighborhood of five hundred. It should be stressed that this estimate is conservative. It is difficult to assess the density of the city's population, which is the most important variable. The number of dead in such a devastating earthquake could have been higher, perhaps a great deal higher.

The 1987 season also turned up corroborating evidence for our ideas about the sequence of earthquakes at Kourion. In room eleven-e, which was part of the open courtyard at the southern edge of the house, we found more wine amphorae from Gaza and painted amphorae with pinched handles similar to those found in room eleven-a. These amphorae are very fragmentary and were used as massive fill after the earlier quake. Because these pots were identical in style to those found in the context of the final quake, we believe that, as we had previously postulated, the earlier quake most likely occurred not long before the great quake that leveled the city—probably twenty to thirty-five years before. Also, the house was shored up and crudely rebuilt and partitioned, but there were no major changes in the area, again suggesting a limited period of time, not multiple occupation phases. This makes our previously considered candidates, the documented Cyprus earthquakes of A.D. 332 and 342, even more attractive.

In the 1987 season, we opened up a whole new area north of the house. The architectural remains we have excavated so far are of such a grand and imposing nature that we have come to believe that this structure must have been a public monument of some sort: we are now calling it the market, because of the shoplike rooms found there. We have excavated masonry blocks and huge ashlars, carved and painted in the Roman Baroque style, weighing up to five hundred pounds each. This building

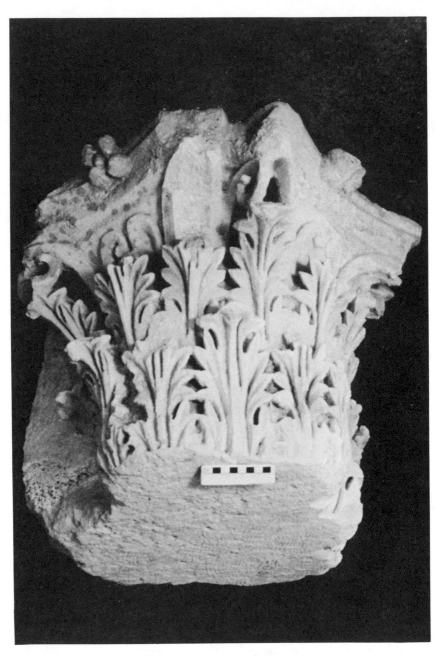

A Corinthian capital from the market still bears traces of its original paint and plaster decoration. (NOELLE SOREN)

was constructed on the southwestern face of the hill, adjoining the much less showy house. The jumbled architectural fragments we have found here include cornice blocks, column shafts, arcuated lintels (flat lintels transformed into carved arches), and four-hundred-pound console blocks. This building was severely rocked by the quake, as evidenced by the fact that the building's facade was tipped twenty degrees.

On the northern edge of the market is an area we have designated room twenty-three, which might have been a storage area. It was entered from the west, from an open area that gave onto the alley that ran behind rooms twenty-five and twenty, where the young Christian family was found. Here we found a fascinating collection of carved half-eggs, eight of glass and two of bone. They were about the size of pigeon eggs and might have been used as counters for a board game, though we have yet to determine of what sort. We also found a curious bronze tool, a little more than a foot long, shaped something like a crocheting needle with hooks at both ends. As is sometimes the case, we may have identified what function this served through a modern analogue: in modern-day Cyprus, a plastic tool quite similar to this one is used for making fishing nets. In addition, an almost identical tool is still used for this purpose by Portuguese fishermen. The mother of Luisa Ferreir Dias, one of the Portuguese archaeologists working on Cyprus, owns one very similar.

We also found two enormous Corinthian capitals here, which we may date by their ornamental detail to the latter first or early second century. Room twenty-three gave access to room twenty-two, a basement adjoining it to the northeast. Here were a number of pots, including an Egyptian amphora, two painted amphorae, and a small jug, as well as a large glass jar that was smashed beyond repair.

Gaming pieces and die from room twenty-eight. (MARTHA COOPER, COURTESY NATIONAL GEOGRAPHIC SOCIETY)

The market, which faced an open square, must have been one of the main gathering places of Kourion, something along the lines of a modern farmer's market. A good deal of the facade, which was of a Roman Baroque style, survives. So far we have recovered twenty large carved blocks that retain varying amounts of their original paint, as well as several rectangular panels in the same colors—predominantly red, yellow, blue, black, and green. The walls inside and out were covered over two stories with geometric frescoes. Their rippling push–pull design shows the influence of the Roman style in southern Turkey, at sites such as Perge and Aspendos.

Pilgrim flask, at left, and Cypriot sigillata plate from room twenty-eight in the market, excavated in 1987. (NOELLE SOREN)

Inside the market we completely excavated two rooms, called twenty-eight and twenty-nine/thirty, which seem to be self-contained shops, though exactly what wares might have been sold there is not yet entirely clear. Room twenty-eight would have been a small, rather elegant shop, with a monumental doorway with plaster molding and an unusually large window looking out on the public square. The walls here, too, were frescoed with geometric designs, which would tend to support the supposition that it was a public place. It was crowded with objects: two local amphorae and the inscribed top of a red-painted amphora, two small jars, a pair of cooking pots, a lamp with rosette decoration, the lower two-thirds of a jug, a shattered glass plate, and sigillata (that is, Roman fineware) plate.

The best clues to the possible identity of the shop were the metal objects: a collection of iron nails, a bronze fishhook, a lead slingshot pellet. There were also about thirty small, cylindrical lead weights, which, it is supposed, were used by fishermen as sinkers for their nets. These items might lead one to suspect that this was a shop catering to fishermen, but in such a thoroughly maritime economy, piscatory implements would not be surprising in any context.

Room twenty-eight contained several mysteries. For one, we found here a collection of more than two hundred small bone tools that look identical to the bobbins used for lacemaking. This discovery is most perplexing—and tantalizing—for the earliest known examples of bobbin lace come from the fifteenth century, more than a thousand years later. Yet bobbins they are, or seem to be, and disbelieving experts have not yet come forward with any other plausible explanation for them.

Here we also found a very beautiful marble baetyl, similar to the ones at the sanctuary of Apollo, though at five inches it is a bit smaller. Because baetyls are known to have existed in classical Cyprus, the existence of this sculpture is no mystery in itself; what is a bit strange is that this icon of pagan religion should have been found in a Christian context. The baetyl was covered with clinging bits of mortar, however, which suggests that the idolatrous sculpture might have been sealed up in the wall, which is certainly consistent with the strictures of early Christianity.

There is some evidence that this room had ceased to function exclusively as a shop after the earlier quake of 332 or 342 and had been converted, like the house next door, to an ad hoc dwelling

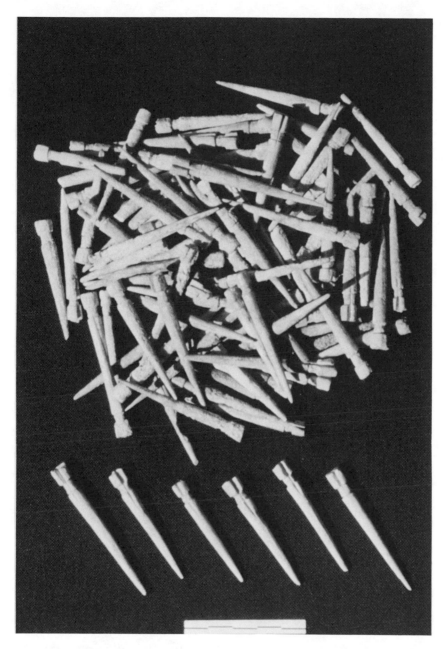

These bone bobbins discovered in the 1987 season may be the earliest evidence yet found of the manufacture of bobbin lace. We believe that they were made at Kourion, because we found one bobbin that was partly carved. (NOELLE SOREN)

This marble baetyl was apparently built into the wall of room twenty-eight of the market. Two more baetyls were found in the Apollo sanctuary. (NOELLE SOREN)

place. In the south corner there was a mud-brick oven, open on one side. A botanical study of the oven's contents has revealed that it was undoubtedly used for baking bread, just as are its modern counterparts. Karen Adams has studied the contents of this and the other ovens we have unearthed at Kourion and has identified charred grains of domesticated wheat, barley, rye, and oats—quite a sophisticated array of grains for this period. Indeed, according to Adams, the contents bear an amazing similarity to a modern loaf of Roman Meal bread.

Next to the oven was a sickle-shaped iron knife with a wooden handle, fastened with bronze, and a straight-edged companion piece, which might have been a whittling knife. In the northern corner was a pithos and a stone grinding bowl set on the floor next to a mud-brick workbench. It was in this area, in the northern part of the trench, that we found our first human skeleton of the season. A male in his early twenties, about five feet four inches in height, he appears to have been lying on the bench at the time of his death. He was on his right side, with his right arm behind his head. He was carrying ten coins on him at the time. Death was caused by the fall of a crushing weight of roof tiles. In view of the early hour of the earthquake, it is reasonable, at least, to postulate that this fellow lived here. It might still have been operating as some sort of shop, with its young proprietor living in.

The shop next door, room thirty, was almost identical, with the same sort of door and large window. There was an arch between the northwest and southeast walls, which the earthquake brought down. At the rear is a little landing that leads up to a back room, which we have labeled room twenty-nine. It has only been partly excavated; so far we have turned up two bronze basins, two pithoi, a bronze ring, and a Gaza amphora. Above room thirty, on the second story, was a loft, room thirty-one, which could have served as a storage room. Access to room thirty-one might have been achieved by ladder. Below it, outside to the east, was an exedra, a small nook in the architecture, with a huge pithos in it. Here there was a little stoa or row of shops along the open space on the northeastern wall.

By the entrance to room thirty, we found one of the most beautiful—and amusing—objects that has yet come to light at Kourion: a bronze hanging lamp in the figure of a duck. The wick is placed in the duck's tail, and the creature is turning its head round to look at its burning bottom! This charming grotesquerie was repaired in antiquity; part of one leg is missing. On the duck's back is a hinged hole through which the lamp's fuel supply is replenished. Amazingly, the hinge still works.

In room thirty we found another skeleton, the remains of a man about thirty years of age. At five feet seven inches in height, he is the most strapping person that we have thus far discovered. He was lying on his left side, with both hands over his face and his legs drawn up. Death occurred when the northwest and northeast walls of the room collapsed upon him. Again, it is a bit difficult to specify what sort of shop this man might have been running, if he was in fact its proprietor. The catalogue of objects recovered here is various: a sickle-shaped knife and a stone grinding bowl, a bronze bowl, two bronze pitchers, a basin with thumb-impressed handles, two pithoi, a bone needle, many iron nails, and a single coin (if he was the shopkeeper, his business had hit a slow patch). Next to the landing leading up to room twenty-nine was a mud-brick workbench with a painted amphora on top of it.

Of course, for any consideration of this room as a shop, the same caveats apply here as in the discussion of room twenty-eight. It might well have been a shop originally, which was converted to a makeshift dwelling after the intermediate earthquake. Or, again, it might still have been a shop, but of an informal nature, with a live-in proprietor.

We unearthed one very strange conundrum in room thirty. There was, in the western corner of the room, by the steps leading to room twenty-nine, a beautifully preserved oven constructed of mud bricks. Part of a curved pithos rim served as an arch over the hole though which the baked goods were taken in and out, and on top of it was a bronze caldron that had caved in the top of the oven, presumably brought down by the impact of the earthquake. Inside the oven we found something absolutely bizarre; a yeti scalp or a cache of Burmese rubies could hardly have produced greater consternation. We found pieces of a plastic bag! Furthermore, one of the pieces of plastic was clearly printed in Greek characters with the name Esel, a department store in the nearby city of Limassol that opened its doors for the first time in 1976. It was not terribly difficult to explain how it got there: there were many holes in the surface here, and big gaps in the massive blocks, which would have made it quite easy for a burrowing rodent to drag that plastic down here sometime during the previous eleven years. Nonetheless, a plastic shopping bag was absolutely the last thing we expected to find in this fourth-century marketplace.

Nor is that the last of the mysteries disclosed in the summer of 1987. One interesting find was a collection of animal bones—cattle, pigs, sheep, and goats—which seem to have been sawed, indicating that they had been butchered for food. The anomaly here, to put it mildly, was the hind foot of a leporid, possibly of the genus *Oryctolagus*, which by all appearances must have belonged to a forty-pound rabbit! Stanley J. Olsen, the zooarchaeologist who accompanied us last season, cautions us that these bones need to be subjected to a careful comparative scrutiny. As is sometimes the case when one confronts a mystery, we can

The human skeleton discovered in room thirty, at five feet seven inches, was the largest victim of the quake we have found thus far. He was attempting to protect his head as the wall fell on him. (NOELLE SOREN)

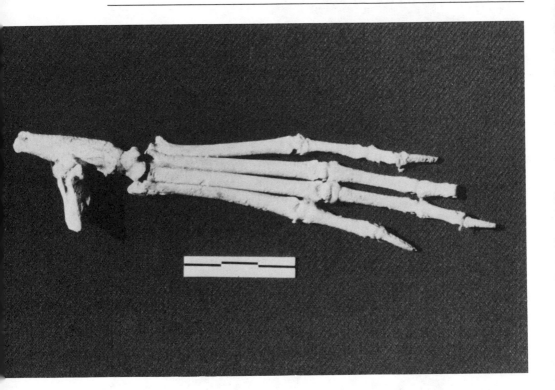

Zoologists believe that this skeletal foot, excavated in the market in 1987, may have belonged to a forty-pound rabbit. (NOELLE SOREN)

do little more than hope that subsequent excavations will shed some light on what it means. Yet nonetheless, there it is, that monstrous rabbit's foot.

Most enigmatic of all (rather creepy, really) are some traces of another human body found just outside room twenty-eight. We have not been able to find enough of them to make even a respectable fragment of a skeleton. A few scant bones that's all, but it shows what awaits us in future excavations.

Far from mysterious, indeed gratifyingly clear, were the inscriptions we found that season on the facade of the market, which constitute explicit corroboration of our prior conjectures about the community at Kourion at the time of the great earthquake of 365. The most charming were casually inscribed letters of the alphabet, including some rather malformed ones, which appear to have been scratched on the wall by a child learning his alphabet. A few graffiti seem to be sums jotted on the wall, perhaps by a shopkeeper figuring his accounts.

Many of the inscriptions are about people of the community: among the personalities who were written about by these ancient graffiti artists are a woman named Demetria, one Sozomenos, and someone called Eutyches, "Lucky," a frequently mentioned name that we have also found on local oil lamps. Another inscription seems to refer to Stadiarches, which means "master of the stadium," close to a modern nickname like "Champ." The only previously attested usage of the word is the name of a bull. More intriguing is an inscription about "the soul of Dionysius." Holt Parker, the epigrapher who puzzled out this information, points out that most of the inscriptions that were excavated in the summer of 1987 broke off in midgraffito, which makes decipherment difficult.

One last inscription, though fragmentary, is crystal clear: scratched into a wall in the marketplace was the phrase "O Jesus . . . of Christ," the ellipsis denoting a lacuna. It is maddening not to have the rest of the graffito, not to know what the ancient scribbler had to say about Jesus. But even standing alone, it is eloquent enough. Perhaps it is from a prayer; more likely it is just part of a simple slogan along the lines of the contemporary "Jesus Saves." Nonetheless, it shows beyond any doubt what we knew in our bones all along: Kourion is a Christian community, and openly so, to permit messages about Jesus to be written in public places. No archaeological find, not even actual physical remains, provides as direct and personal a connection as graffiti, for there is no activity more uniquely human than writing. When we see the message a person has scratched on the wall, we are being communicated with directly, without any kind of intermediary, scholarly or imaginative. Was this message written here by a mystical preacher? a pious little girl? perhaps someone cursing? We shall never know exactly who it was scribbled that graffito, but the world in which the writer lived is coming to life in crisp and startling detail.

PART TWO

A HISTORICAL SKETCH OF KOURION

IT SOMETIMES SURPRISES even people quite well versed in history to find out just how thriving and various a place antiquity was. It is easy, when reading history books, to fall into the fallacy of thinking of Thebes and Babylon and Jerusalem and Athens and the other great seats of ancient culture as shining turreted metropolises separated by endless miles of wasteland, traversed only by caravans making the trek from one city to the next. This prejudice perhaps grows out of the irresistible tendency of modern culture to center itself in great cities. In fact, antiquity was not a particularly urban place. With the exception of Rome, the better-known ancient capitals were small cities even by the standards of the Middle Ages; and a place like Kourion, which was never very populous, regardless of which empire happened to be its overlord at a particular moment, had a vital cultural life of its own.

In fact, Kourion was by any standard a very ancient city. There had been a settlement there from the earliest Bronze Age, as attested by some tombs found in a settlement called Bamboula, in the modern village of Episkopi. Then, sometime in the thirteenth or twelfth century B.C., a colony was established in Kourion by Mycenaean Greeks. This is quite a hoary tradition, cited by no less an authority than Herodotus, the first historian, who tells us that Kourion was a colony founded by Greeks from Argos. However, it is quite possible, as we shall see, that this reference to the Argives was a bit of ax-grinding on Herodotus's part and that it ought to be taken loosely to mean simply "Greek," which at this period would be identified with Mycenae (in any case, Argos and Mycenae were only seven miles apart). Homer, too, uses "Argive" and "Achaean," not to mention "Danaan," with apparent impartiality as synonyms for what were later called the Hellenes and are to us, simply, Greeks.

The Mycenaean colony must have been successful, for it was known as far away as Egypt. In an inscription at the Egyptian temple of Medinet Habu, Kourion appears (or so it would seem) on a list of the kingdoms that the great Pharaoh Rameses III (1198–1166 B.C.) was eyeing for possible conquest. Caution is necessary, however, because the decipherment of hieroglyphs is nowhere near as certain a matter as is generally supposed. The question is whether one can equate what would be transliterated as *Kir* with Kourion, yet even so careful a historian as Sir George Hill does so, confidently, in his definitive *History of Cyprus.*

One of the most intriguing archaeological sites of the Mycenaean world is located at Kourion: a royal tomb in a place called Kaloriziki, a seaside settlement at the foot of the cliff upon which sits the city of Kourion. In 1903 or thereabouts (some uncertainty exists about the exact date, but George Mc-Fadden gives this date) grave robbers from Episkopi broke into the tomb and made off with some well-preserved pots, beautifully wrought bronze urn handles and tripods, and the most important item, an exquisite gold and cloisonné enameled scepter, a staff surmounted with a sphere upon which perch two carefully sculptured hawks. It is the oldest example of true cloisonné enamelwork in the Mediterranean, preceding by many centuries the use of the technique in Egypt. Partly for this reason, a much later date was for years assigned to the tomb.

The regal tomb of Kaloriziki has prompted a great deal of speculation, some of it quite fanciful. The most brilliantly colored of these theories is that put forth by George McFadden. In one of his very last archaeological adventures, he rediscovered the tomb fifty years after it had originally been rifled, based on information from the last surviving member of the grave-robbing gang. Following directions straight out of *Treasure Island* ("The tomb, he [the grave robber] said, was on the scarp between a fig tree and a carob tree with three trunks and close to a wild hawthorn"), McFadden unearthed many artifacts that the Cypriot grave robbers had left behind, including the rather spectacular find of fragments, in the form of the bronze bosses, of a Mycenaean shield, which could be reconstructed as an example of the type represented on the famous "Warrior Vase" of Mycenae. It was the first such shield ever found and established beyond doubting the provenance and antiquity of the tomb.

McFadden's theory about the identity of the shield's owner is based on the fact that the remains found here, most likely a man and a woman, were cremated, a funeral practice almost unknown on Cyprus in the twelfth century B.C. Nor was incineration at all common in Mycenae. McFadden supposed that the person whose ashes were here interred was a warrior king (that they are royal relics is established by the presence of the scepter), who had learned the practice on the battlefield of the Trojan War! In an article in the *American Journal of Archaeology*, published in 1954, McFadden writes, "Cremation was practised in Troy VI and presumably also in VII A, and if this was the city sacked by the Achaians as narrated by Homer, we may assume that the Achaians who practised the custom on the field of battle at Troy borrowed it from the Trojans and, after the fall of Troy and during the unsettled conditions preceding and following the destruction of Mycenae, introduced it elsewhere."

His chain of reasoning is admirably streamlined, untroubled by any vexatious doubts about the historicity of the Trojan War. He skips lightly over the most sweeping "if" clauses imaginable: "If the scepter-bearing king was at Troy and learnt cremation there, let us say that he was twenty-five years of age at the time of the fall of the city in 1180 B.C., the lowest likely date for this event, which should precede the invasion of Egypt by the sea people." McFadden's interpretation is wonderfully romantic, and no one could prove it wrong: nonetheless, suffice it to say that there is too little secure information about these virtually prehistoric events to confirm it. When McFadden wrote, in 1954, many scholars were seduced by the admittedly seductive idea that in the *Iliad* Homer was versifying about a real war, as opposed to myth. Schliemann and his followers had adduced much evidence to support that view. There was never a consensus on the subject, however, and certainly nowadays most classicists do not advise teaching Homer in the history curriculum. Still, McFadden *might* be right. Another hypothesis, hardly less romantic, is that a Mycenaean king died on the high sea, and his crew made an unscheduled landfall at Kourion for his obsequies.

At any rate, the enameled scepter found in the tomb at Kaloriziki is the most important national treasure of modern Cyprus. It was on permanent display at the Cyprus Museum in Nicosia until the Turkish invasion and subsequent partition of the island, at which time the museum's curators removed it, for fear that it might be stolen for political purposes. It is still hidden somewhere in Nicosia.

Kourion also shows up in an Assyrian inscription dated about the turn of the seventh century B.C. as one of the seven kingdoms of Cyprus. Epigraphers are in conflict about the exact date and meaning of the inscription, which was found on a stele at Kition (modern Larnaca) and is now on display in Berlin. The inscription, apparently dating from 673 or 672 B.C., seems to be saying that in 708 B.C. the King of Kourion, one Eteandros, was summoned to Nineveh to pay homage to the Assyrian king, Sargon II, who was levying the Cypriot kingdoms for the contribution of building materials for his great new palace at Nineveh.

Kourion next appears, quite ignobly, in Herodotus's chronicle of one of many wars fought between the Greeks and the Persians over control of Cyprus. A certain Onesilus, the King of Salamis and hero of the story, organized the Cypriot princes into an alliance with the Ionian Greeks and led them in an uprising against the Persian overlords. About 499 B.C. the battle was pitched at Amathus, which had refused to join the revolt; Onesilus led the combined Cypriot and Ionian forces in a siege against the Persian sympathizers. Kourion, however, betrayed the cause, turning even Onesilus's own men against him. According to Herodotus, writing some fifty years after the fact, "Stesenor, the ruler of Kourion (Kourion is said to have been a colony from Argos), with a considerable body of troops under his command, played traitor; and his lead was immediately followed by the war chariots from Salamis. The result was a victory for Persia, and in the rout of the Cyprian army many were killed, including Onesilus, the son of Chersis and originator of the Cyprian revolt."

The people of Amathus took their revenge on the corpse of Onesilus, severing its head and mounting it on a pike above the city gates. This head in time became hollow and a swarm of bees moved into it and created a honeycomb. The Amathusians consulted an oracle, Herodotus tells us, "and were advised to take the head down and bury it, and, if they wished to prosper, to regard Onesilus thenceforward as a hero, and to honor him with an annual sacrifice. This was done, and the ceremony was still observed in my own day." Most telling is the little parenthetical phrase about Kourion having been founded by Argos. It is placed in the very middle of the sentence that describes the treachery of the Kourians under Stesenor; clearly, the reader is meant to identify villainy with these Persian sympathizers, while the honors and glory go ultimately to Onesilus, who was steadfastly loyal to the Greeks. It seems that among the Greeks at this time there was a great deal of controversy surrounding Argos, many of them regarding the Argives as secretly siding with the hated Persian enemy under Darius. Thus Herodotus, a thoroughly red-blooded Greek, casually inserts the statement that the Kourians are Argives by descent as the explanation of their treacherous behavior.

In the next century, Kourion once again joins forces with the Greeks, its King Pasikrates sending ships and men to aid Alexander the Great in his siege of Tyre. After that the city disappears from the historical record for quite a long span of time—indeed, for most of the period covered by the greatest portion of the modern archaeology of the city. This silence does not mean that Kourion was in decline. Excavations at the sanctuary of Apollo and at the city site suggest the opposite, though there is some evidence of a falloff in the later Hellenistic period. The important point is that Kourion was apparently able to stay out of the continuing military struggle for control of Cyprus and the endless seesawing of intrainsular alliances, and could concentrate on its importance as a religious pilgrimage center.

Then Cyprus again came into the Mediterranean spotlight in the very earliest days of the Christian church, when Paul and Barnabas arrived there on their first mission abroad. According to the author of the Acts of the Apostles, they went through the isle to Paphos, where they found "a certain sorcerer, a false prophet, a Jew, whose name was Bar-jesus," who was with the Roman governor, Sergius Paulus, "a prudent man." The latter called the missionary preachers to him to hear what they had to say, but the sorcerer Bar-jesus tried to turn them away, a fatal error. Paul, "filled with the Holy Ghost, set his eyes on him," delivered a withering invective against him, and blinded him. "And immediately there fell on [Bar-jesus] a mist and a darkness; and he went about seeking some to lead him by the hand." Understandably impressed, Sergius Paulus converted on the spot.

The author of the Acts tells us no more about the Cypriot ministry, but another book, the Acts of Barnabas the Apostle, fleshes out the story. This history, the manuscript of which is at the Vatican, is now all but forgotten, and is only published in the encyclopedic nineteenth-century Acta Sanctorum. It tells us what Paul and Barnabas did on their way to that triumph against Bar-jesus at Paphos. The forty-fourth chapter of the

Acts of Barnabas, which is narrated by some anonymous fol-
lower of the apostles, may be translated as follows:

> There was a certain cursed highway into the mountain near that
> city we have seen celebrated [Paphos]. There, a multitude of naked
> men and women were having their exercises on this trail. When
> Barnabas saw this, he whirled around in his tracks and reproached
> them. Immediately, that part of the mountain facing east sank, and
> many people were injured, and many among them died. The rest
> took refuge in the temple of Apollo, which was nearby. Indeed,
> when we had come near the place called Kourion, a great multi-
> tude of Jews, stirred up by that man Bar-jesus, stood outside the
> city and did not permit us to enter there. But we passed the night
> at the foot of an oak tree, which is on the mountain near that city,
> and there we were refreshed.

The most compelling aspect of this passage—certainly its
most prophetic part—is that Barnabas, in his righteous indig-
nation at what sound like jogging nudists ("mulierum et
virorum multitudo nudis corporibus cursum exercebat")
wreaked what sounds very much like an earthquake near the
sanctuary of Apollo. The main reason this momentous event
seems not to have made it into the canonical Acts of the Apostles is that it features Barnabas, not Paul, as the thaumaturge.

Nevertheless, after they had gone on to Paphos and scored
their great triumph over that wicked, troublemaking Bar-jesus,
Paul and Barnabas returned to the mainland, sailing to Asia
Minor, where their evangelical partnership continued for a
while longer. They had a notable adventure in Lystra, in ancient Lycaonia, where their miracle-working ways caused the
populace to think they were gods. The Lystrans mistook Paul,
the spokesman, for Mercury, but Barnabas they took to be Jupi-
ter, father of the gods.

Soon thereafter, in Antioch, the two apostles quarreled and

parted company. Barnabas wanted to bring along with them on their next journey his kinsman, the apostle Mark, who, tradition holds, went on to write the second gospel. But for reasons left unstated by the author of the Acts, Paul objected to this arrangement. The partnership broke up. Paul headed north with his new sidekick, Silas, and Barnabas went home to Cyprus, taking Mark with him.

Barnabas was one of the most remarkable and accomplished of the early church fathers, yet he seems not to have had as efficacious a publicity campaign as the other apostles. Christian tradition, as embodied by the New Testament canon, has a marked Paulist and Petrine bias, and to track the career of the Cypriot apostle after he left Paul, one must ransack obscure ecclesiastical documents. As one reads the "official" Acts of the Apostles, up to the point that they separated, Barnabas and Paul seemed to have been peers. Yet after the split Barnabas disappears altogether, and the author follows Paul (whose missions, indeed, were unquestionably the most important of Christianity's early days).

Nonetheless, Barnabas was a busy man: it is well attested that he founded the Church of Milan on a journey with Mark to Italy soon after his return to Cyprus, and it appears quite possible that he founded the Church of Rome. On this Italian tour, Barnabas went first to Milan, in A.D. 52, the year he established the church there. He went to Rome in 54, immediately after Nero came to the throne (Claudius, Nero's predecessor, had enforced a decree that prohibited Jews from entering the city). This date makes it seem very likely that he preceded Peter, whom we are able to place in Antioch until 55. Thus the Holy See of Rome might well have been founded not by the Prince of the Apostles but by a quarrelsome Cypriot Jew.

Official ecclesiastical history, however, has always depended heavily on the concept of apostolic succession, the church's authority proceeding directly from Jesus to Peter: "[T]hou art Peter, and upon this rock I will build my church; and the gates of hell shall not prevail against it. And I will give unto thee the keys of the kingdom of heaven" (Matthew 16:18–19). Thus the church derives its power from Peter, from whom flows divine authority directly down to all the popes and bishops since. It is easy to understand that orthodoxy would have squelched the notion that a far less famous apostle, one from an out-of-the-way place like Cyprus, who was furthermore on the outs with St. Paul, beat out Peter in establishing the mother church.

Because of the very obscurity of St. Barnabas, it is not at all easy to get to the bottom of this question. Here is an example of how recondite are the sources pertaining to Barnabas: for one of the vital bits of evidence dealing with his claim to the founding of the church in Rome, one must consult a quite rare nineteenth-century pamphlet by the Reverend F. D. Harriman, M.A., entitled "The Career of Barnabas After St. Paul Left Him," wherein is quoted an abridgment of William Cave's *Lives of the Primitive Fathers.* This piece was appended to *The Apostolic Fathers,* an eighteenth-century translation by William Wake, the Archbishop of Canterbury, of a historical work by one Charles Burton. Once found, however, the quotation from Cave in Harriman's pamphlet is instructive:

> "Dorotheus [sixth-century Syrian jurist] and the author of the Recognitions [third-century Christian didactic fiction], and some other writings attributed to St. Clement, make him (Barnabas) to have been at Rome, and one of the first that preached the Christian faith in that city: for which Baronius (a Roman Catholic historian in the time of Elizabeth), falls foul upon them, not being willing that any should be thought to have been there before St. Peter,

though after him (and it is but good manners to let him go first), he is not unwilling to grant his being there."

The important part of that quotation, aside from the fact that several early Christian writers thought that Barnabas had a prior claim, is the parenthetical statement that good manners compel one nonetheless to grant priority to St. Peter. It is quite difficult to say whose opinion is being expressed here—the original Cave, the quoted Burton (in Wake's translation), or the Reverend Harriman, who neglected to put it in brackets. In any case, the modern reader may disagree and be of the opinion that, on the contrary, good manners have nothing whatever to do with it, and there is rather a more compelling interest in getting at the historical truth. If we give Harriman's punctuation the benefit of the doubt and attribute the sentiment to the archbishop's rendering of Mr. Burton's book, then we may gloss the remark thus: "No point in making trouble with official Rome by casting aspersions on the primacy of their first primate." In any case, the quester for historical accuracy will likely go unsatisfied, as Barnaban studies, at the moment, approach nil.

Harriman in his pamphlet conjectures that Barnabas after his Italian expedition went to North Africa and founded the church in Carthage. According to the usually reliable Tertullian, an early church father, Barnabas was the author of the Epistle to the Hebrews, "a letter of warning, exhortation, and consolation," according to Harriman. "This letter was probably written at Carthage; and, though not intended for that city, a copy of it, signed with the author's name, seems to have been left there." Barnabas left another copy of it with his friend, St. Clement of Rome (who, it will be remembered, was one of those who testified on Barnabas's behalf as the founder of the church there). Despite the clear weight of evidence supporting Barnabas's authorship, the Epistle to the Hebrews remains officially anonymous. The bias against the Cypriot apostle seems to be quite stubborn. The one ecclesiastical document ascribed to him, the Epistle of Barnabas, clearly was not written by him. Harriman writes: "To the injury of denying his authorship of the great Epistle to the Hebrews has been added the insult of ascribing to him that later and inferior production, the so-called 'Epistle of Barnabas'—that absurd epistle, which says, among other strange things, that the hyaena every year changes its sex, and is sometimes male and sometimes female."

Little more information survives about Barnabas, except that he died on Cyprus, his native island. Tradition holds that he was martyred, but it does not specify the method. His relics have provided much interest over the years.

After the Saracens occupied Cyprus in the seventh century, the head and other relics of Barnabas were translated to Milan, one of the churches he founded. A rival body of Barnabas, found in Constantinople in the early ninth century, now resides in Toulouse at the Church of St. Saturninus. The *Gallican Martyrology* states that "the head is now exposed there to veneration, apart from the body, which reposes in its own shrine." However, according to the Reverend Sabine Baring-Gould, in his *Lives of the Saints*, "the Church of Edna, in the district of Bergamo claims to possess the head of S. Barnabas; at Pavia are particles of bone from the head; in Genoa, in the cathedral, the head entire; a jaw at Cremona; some bones in the cathedral of Tournai; the head entire, and a rib at Andechs in Bavaria, part of the head at Prague, the head entire also in the Jesuit Church at Naples, a leg at Florence." Concludes Baring-Gould, "There is some strange error which demands investigation in the matter of the relics of S. Barnabas."

After the great earthquake of A.D. 365, Kourion sank into the earth and was completely forgotten for a generation, until a new wave of Christian settlers gradually repopulated the abandoned site. It may seem passing strange to us in the Information Age that a city, formerly of such importance, could lapse into utter obscurity. To understand why, it is necessary to consider just how disastrous the earthquake was: it is quite possible that there were no survivors at all, not only in Kourion itself but in environs lying at some miles' distance. Those who did survive the earthquake found themselves in a place more or less uninhabitable and must have moved off quickly to a more hospitable environment. Once deserted, the city would have soon been covered by the sand that continually blows up from the adjacent beach.

Another important point to consider in examining how Kourion came to be desolated and left intact is our hypothesis that the inhabitants at the time of the quake were not prosperous and established merchants, who would have left behind shops and houses attractive to scavengers, but poor Christian settlers. If our conception of Kourion at the time of the earthquake is correct, most of its inhabitants were itinerant squatters, perhaps from some distant place, who would not have had relatives coming in search of them. The district might soon have acquired a reputation for being an uninhabitable wreck, overrun with rats, offering neither shelter nor treasure. As time went by, and the sand continued inexorably to accrete, the city could very easily have been forgotten and left deserted for years. This conclusion, at least, is the natural one in view of the physical evidence.

Thus, when the city gradually began to be repopulated, beginning about twenty years (a full generation) later, it was essentially a new settlement. Although, as we shall see, a good deal of masonry was cannibalized from classical structures for the postquake Christian Kourion, most of the buildings were entirely new. This last wave of settlement would have been aware that the ruins of an old city were around but must have seen in them nothing worth digging up. We have no written records from this period of the city's history, so it is to a certain extent guesswork. Yet, again, the physical evidence is overwhelming that the buildings we have excavated in the city of Kourion were untouched in the years after the great earthquake.

This era of established Christianity (which we shall treat in some detail later on), beginning at the end of the fourth century and lasting into the seventh century, was Kourion's final period of prosperity. The fatal blow to the city occurred when the local bishopric moved its seat to the neighboring village, Episkopi, the name of which attests to its ecclesiastical origins. The reasons for the final abandonment of Kourion cannot be identified beyond a doubt; it may have partly been due to the fact that Episkopi had a better and more reliable water supply. Yet the primary cause must have been the raids by Arab marauders that began in the seventh century.

Situated so advantageously—and so conspicuously—on its cliff above the Mediterranean Sea, Kourion was a rich prize for the Islamic adventurers. In the words of J. Nicolas Coldstream, in his essay on the history of Cyprus, "Misery and chaos descended upon the island soon after the advent of Islam." The professor might have added that strife between Christian and Muslim has never ceased to affect the people of Cyprus right down to the present day.

Just as it had been in ancient times, Cyprus was again a bone of contention between opposing empires. For more than three hundred years, beginning with the sack of Salamis in 648, the island was raped and plundered by roving Arab raiders based in their strongholds in Egypt and the Levant. Rule of Cyprus during this epoch changed at least eleven times, and the island was occasionally subject to the Byzantine Emperor and the Umayyad Caliph at the same time—thus having to pay tribute to them both. In the words of Willibald of Eichstätt, an English pilgrim who visited Paphos in the eighth century, "Cyprus lived between the Greeks and the Saracens."

The suffering of the Cypriots at the hands of the Arab raiders from the seventh through the tenth centuries was frightful. Multitudes were slaughtered, many more taken as captives and brought to Arab territories as slaves, including on one occasion, it is said, the Archbishop. In 692 Emperor Justinian II had the well-intentioned but rather misguided idea of resettling the wretched Cypriots in a new city on the Sea of Marmara, which was called, naturally, Justinianopolis. In commemoration of this event, modern archbishops of Cyprus still bear the title "Archbishop of Nova Justiniana and all Cyprus." This Byzantine experiment in utopianism was abandoned after six years, but not without provoking yet another Arab invasion of Cyprus.

This raid, which probably occurred in 698 (there exists some confusion about the date among the various authorities, but this date is preferred by Professor Coldstream), left the major positive contribution of the Arabs on the island, the Hala Sultan Tékké. Otherwise known as the Tékké (which means shrine) of Umm Haram, this superbly romantic mosque and minaret, surrounded by a grove of ancient palm trees at the edge of a salt lake, is one of the most sacred sites in all of Islam, ranking immediately after the shrines of Mecca and Medina. It contains the remains of Umm Haram, the maternal aunt of

Muhammad, who, while accompanying her husband on the raid, fell off the ass she was riding. According to one Islamic chronicler, she immediately "broke her pellucid neck and yielded up her victorious soul, and in that fragrant spot was at once buried." Her grave is the site of the mosque, which was not completed until 1816 by the then Turkish governor of Cyprus. It used to be customary for Turkish ships when they passed by the *tékké* to dip their flags and fire a salute. It is situated virtually within walking distance of the airport at Larnaca, and (in the language of guidebooks) is on no account to be missed.

There were more and more ferocious raids—in 743, 773, 790, and 806—the last, waged by Harun al-Rashid, being particularly ruinous. While in the accounts of the Arab attacks it is difficult to match the cities sacked with the particular raid, it is safe to state that a famous episcopal seat like Kourion, with its beautifully decorated basilica and bishop's residence, would have been an obvious target and was most likely pillaged several times.

Kourion was not the only coastal city abandoned for a more defensible inland location. At Paphos, for example, while a few hardy souls remained on the littoral and built a massive castle called Saranta Kolones to fortify their position, most of the Paphians retreated to the headlands, establishing the settlement called Ktima. That explains why the modern city of Paphos is so densely populated several kilometers inland, while the beach area is very thinly settled.

By the time the raids were finally squelched, in 964, by Emperor Nikephoros II Phokas, Kourion had progressed far along its irresistible slide into obscurity, just as Cyprus itself finally experienced an interval, lasting a few centuries, of peace and relative geopolitical irrelevance. Quite happily, no doubt, as far as the islanders were concerned, Cyprus drifted ever more profoundly into insignificance, first as a minor dependency of the late Byzantine Empire, until 1191, when Richard Coeur de Lion conquered it (and got married in Limassol) on his way to the Third Crusade, then as a Lusignan dependency, and finally as a Venetian colony, this latter period now chiefly remembered for Shakespeare's Othello, who was governor there.

Yet by this time, Kourion was not just obscure: it was a broken, forgotten ruin. For the next thousand years, more or less, the story of the city was the slow accretion of dirt and sand.

Yet time, in that way that it has, finally brought around the nineteenth century and with it the vogue for amateur archaeology. Upper-class Victorian gentlemen, ever in need of a self-improving fad, swarmed over the Mediterranean, on the lookout for buried cities. Happily unencumbered by the demands of scientific observation and motivated by the hope of finding golden treasures for their drawing rooms, or perhaps a case in the British Museum bearing their name, these eager dilettantes were suddenly to be found in every place that had ever laid a claim to a classical pedigree.

The glory that was Kourion had long since been effaced, of course, but there did remain a few Ozymandian traces of its former regal and sacred status: a romantic scatter of broken columns, a weedy stretch of rutted pavement, a semicircular depression in the ground that might have been a Roman theater. The local shepherds and citrus farmers called a rocky eminence high on a seaside cliff (the place that had once been the sanctuary of Apollo) by the suspiciously classical name of "Apellon."

Just the thing, in other words, to catch the eye of someone like the American consul in Nicosia, General Emmanuele Pietro Paolo Maria Luigi Palma di Cesnola, Civil War hero, member of the Royal Academy of Sciences, Turin, the first excavator of Kourion and humbug extraordinaire. Born in the Italian village of Rivarolo Canavese, near Turin, in 1832, Cesnola served as a teenaged officer in the Austrian War of 1848 and in the Crimean War. In 1860, he emigrated to the United States and founded a military school at the corner of Broadway and Twenty-second Street in New York City. He served in the Civil War as a colonel for the Fourth Volunteer Cavalry of New York. At the Battle of Aldie (Virginia), Cesnola raised such a ruckus when an officer junior to himself was promoted over him that he was placed under arrest. When the men under his command were ordered into battle, they refused to budge until their hotheaded Italian commander was released from confinement.

He then led a charge on the Confederate position, in which he was seriously wounded, a deed he later called "a foolhardy and reckless act." He was captured by the Confederates and held as a prisoner of war, though his confinement appears not to have been too rigorous. In one letter to his wife he asked her to send him bologna and macaroni for his soup. After the war, President Lincoln, just days before his assassination, appointed him to the post of American consul in Cyprus.

Cesnola landed at Larnaca on Christmas Day 1865. Things began rather awkwardly: his wife, a respectable Victorian lady, refused to disembark, because there was no "proper conveyance," and she naturally refused the Cypriot stevedores' scandalous offer to carry her on their shoulders. The impasse was only resolved when the local hearties waded out to the ship with a chair for her. It is not at all surprising that Cesnola was soon drawn into the great Victorian treasure hunt. His English and French counterparts in Cyprus, as well as the English director of the Ottoman Bank in Larnaca, were all employed in digging up the island, and Cesnola did not delay in hiring his own crew of local workmen and commencing to dig. Even by the standards of the day, he was hugely successful.

At the turn of the century, John L. Myres, an Oxonian art historian, wrote in his handbook to the Cesnola collection at the Metropolitan Museum of Art: "He seems to have secured in an unusual degree the good will of the peasantry and native excavators, and to have had prompt information of chance finds all over the island; and in eleven busy years he amassed what is still the largest, and in many respects the richest collection of Cypriote antiquities in the world." Myres rather cattily goes on to say, "Its value would have been even greater, had the conditions of discovery been more favorable to scientific record." In other words, had Cesnola done something more than merely washing things off and carting them away for sale abroad.

Cesnola's house in Larnaca was an impromptu museum of his discoveries and one of the principal attractions on the island. To his dismay, he became aware of tourists, "apparently respectable, who think nothing of pocketing antiquities not belonging to them." It seems almost churlish to point out the irony of these words coming from a man who excavated, by one count, 35,573 objects, which he took abroad as his personal property and sold for considerable sums of money. When the Grand Vizier of Constantinople tried to prevent Cesnola from taking some of his antiquities out of Cyprus (the island being at the time a part of the Ottoman Empire), the American consul asked Washington to send him a Navy man-of-war, which they obligingly did, for the purpose of removing his collection.

It is common to hear lamentations about the woeful inadequacy of the field techniques used by archaeologists of Cesnola's day, and complaints about their indiscriminate and highly immoral acquisitiveness. Nonetheless, in fairness to Cesnola and company, it must be pointed out that they found formidable competition in the native grave robbers, who showed not a whit less cupidity in their wholesale emptying of ancient tombs. And if it is true that the Cesnolas of the latter nineteenth century did not anticipate scientific techniques that were only beginning to be developed, at least we have their highly colorful and romantic accounts of their journeys.

And Cesnola was nothing if not colorful and romantic. His published writings about his expeditions in Cyprus are real page turners, in the spirit of the adventure stories for boys so popular in his day. Cesnola had a real flair for breathless narrative, which uncannily anticipates the pulp fiction and B movies of our century that take buried cities and sunken treasures as their theme. Indeed, in approaching a book like his lavishly illustrated *Cyprus: Its Ancient Cities, Tombs, and Temples*, it is a difficult problem to determine where one must leave off being skeptical and simply disbelieve everything. Here, for example, he provides an excellent description of Kourion's appearance in 1865, a trifle flowery, to be sure, but which nonetheless has a trustworthy ring (and, perhaps more to the point, can be verified in part by modern observation):

> I counted seven spots where shafts of columns, either in marble or granite, are lying half buried in the ground, probably in the same position as when they fell centuries ago! In one place there are stone steps quite worn out by the busy feet which came and went to a cistern near by, where the Rebeccas of Curium [the Latin form of Kourion, commonly used in the nineteenth century] resorted to fill their water jars at evening, and talk over the news and scandal of the day. In another spot a large diota [a type of amphora]

lies broken beneath a rectangular stone, as undisturbed as if the crash had occurred but yesterday. Broken lamps, and handles of a diota inscribed, a large millstone with a copper ring rivetted into it, and everywhere masses of broken pottery strew the ground. Now and then parts of the street pavement are visible, marked with the tracks of chariot wheels, and altogether the scene is one which fires the imagination to conjure up the ancient days of the city.

Now, even if Cesnola's conjectures about the scandal-ridden conversations of the Rebeccas of Curium are not particularly useful to us, his full description of the site as it was 120 years ago is really invaluable; the diota crushed under the stone, for example, sounds very much like an event of the earthquake, undisturbed for over a thousand years. Furthermore, Cesnola's account shows us that in the seventy years intervening between his exploration and the first scientific expedition here, the Penn group supervised by George McFadden, Kourion was buried under several feet of sandy soil.

Then Cesnola's narrative shifts seamlessly into fantasy. He laboriously describes his excavation of one sector of the city, exactly which one he does not say. First, he removed some broken columns, beneath which he found a beautiful mosaic floor in a lotus pattern. The mosaic was broken up, not by the falling of the broken columns, he says, but by a treasure seeker's spade. He does not explain how he arrived at this conclusion. Underneath the broken mosaic he found a layer of charcoal two feet thick, and beneath that another stratum of sand. Now he goes on to say that he decided to dig farther down, "inasmuch as it sounded quite hollow." It remains mysterious to a modern digger how a heap of broken mosaic cubes, resting upon a bed of charcoal and sand, could sound hollow, but dig he did, and "some twenty feet deeper than the treasure hunter had gone," he discovered a gallery carved into the limestone. After it had been partly excavated, a door leading to another room was found. "I descended into the first chamber for the purpose of examining it, and while poking into the remaining earth with my foot-rule, I struck something hard, which turned out to be a bracelet, with several other gold objects in a small heap."

A third, and then a fourth treasure chamber was found. The more Cesnola dug, the more marvelous gold antiquities his spade turned up: "During the several days employed in exploring Room C," he tells us, "I remained in it the whole time, and every object was discovered in my presence. Scarcely a moment passed without some gold ornament being brought to light." Pages and pages in his book catalogue the immense haul from these underground rooms, which Cesnola opined was not a tomb at all but treasure chambers attached to the temple above. He called it the Treasure of Curium, and he became an international celebrity, something very much to his taste. John Taylor Johnston, president of the fledgling Metropolitan Museum and one of the cultural lions of New York, called the haul "the most precious single discovery of ancient art ever made."

It is great stuff, this tale of the dashing general, "the indefatigable and accomplished explorer," and his treasure chambers. The only hitch is that it is all a lie. The "Treasure of Curium" is one of the most elaborate hoaxes in art history: the careful measurements of the "treasure chambers," the wealth of realistic anecdotal narration, were pure invention from the egomaniacal brain of the ambitious general. The extent of his ambition may be judged from the following excerpt from a letter he wrote to a friend back in the States: "Your friend Cesnola has just made the discovery of many gold things, beneath a Temple here; the quantity and quality of which throws into shade Schliemann's so-called 'Treasure of Priam.' "

As Myres tactfully puts it in his handbook, "The famous 'Treasure of Curium,' circumstantially described in Chapter XI of his book, is a mystery that cannot be cleared up. All attempts to locate the treasure chambers of which Cesnola gives us a plan in his book have failed, and the occurrence of objects of so many different periods in the 'Treasure' itself is very difficult to coordinate with our other knowledge of ancient Cyprus." No one could find the chambers, of course, because they never existed. And the explanation of the heterogeneity of the treasure is that Cesnola dug the pieces up all over Cyprus. Some of the items, apparently, he bought from antique dealers.

Nonetheless, at the time no one doubted that they were dealing with anything less than the greatest collection of antiquities in the world. The British Museum offered Cesnola fifty thousand dollars in gold, the Louvre sixty thousand; but he wanted his collection to go to his adopted country, so he cabled the Metropolitan, offering to sell it to them on favorable terms (though not reducing the price). They raised the money and the bogus treasure went to the New World. "All right!" cabled the general in reply, "three cheers for our dear New York museum." Later that year, while he was supervising the uncrating and cataloguing of his collection, the trustees asked him to become the museum's first director. He accepted, and ruled over the palace in Central Park as an autocrat for nearly thirty stormy years.

The most turbulent storm of his directorship came in 1880, when the journal *Art Amateur* published an article accusing Cesnola of having foisted off fraudulent artworks on the museum: ironically, the works in question were not from the Treasure of Curium and were in fact genuine. The attack was written by Gaston L. Feuardent, the son of a Parisian art dealer with whom Cesnola was having an ongoing feud. The trustees of the museum advised Cesnola to keep his cool, but he flew into a towering Italianate rage, referring to the attack as a piece by "the French Jew dealer Feuardent in an obscure monthly paper edited by a Jew." The obscure monthly paper he thereafter referred to as *Art Defamateur*. The trial, a page-one scandal in the New York press, had more than a hint of anti-Semitism to it, as Cesnola's remark suggests. After ninety-two days of deliberation, the jury exonerated the furious and falsely maligned collector.

In its official history, the Metropolitan portrays Cesnola as a far from brilliant director for the museum. His later years seem to be noted principally by the fierceness with which he resisted efforts to force him into retirement. Nonetheless, Cesnola left his mark on Cyprus: when we were digging at the sanctuary of Apollo during our first season there, we found a tomb well to the east of the archaic precinct. It was dirty and cobwebby and crawling with the large, nimble spiders that inhabit Cyprus, but we persevered in clearing it out in the hopes of finding human remains and the usual accompanying ceramics and votive offerings. Someone had beaten us to it, however. The tomb was empty, or almost: when we got to the back of the tomb, we found a *tabula ansata*, a particularly elegant sort of graffito, carefully carved into the soft limestone of the interior wall. In the middle of it was inscribed, in lovely nineteenth-century italic script: "L.P.C. 1875." Luigi Palma di Cesnola, like many another Victorian tourist, had left behind a memento; or perhaps it was a bit of braggadocio so that we would know who had cheated us of our treasure, a joke that waited a hundred years for the other shoe to drop.

This photograph, taken about 1935, shows work in progress at the sanctuary of Apollo dig conducted by the University of Pennsylvania. The photograph looks down the main street in front of the temple of Apollo. George McFadden stands by the trench at upper right, his hands behind his back. (COURTESY OF ROGER EDWARDS, UNIVERSITY OF PENNSYLVANIA MUSEUM)

The next wave of excavation, as we have seen, came in the thirties, under the direction of George McFadden. We have had much to say about McFadden, and little remains to be added. Christofis Polycarpou, who has served our expedition well as the principal liaison between the Americans and the Cypriots, knew and worked with McFadden. He describes him as popular and even well loved. While McFadden never achieved any great measure of fame as an archaeologist, he nonetheless seems to have been tremendously popular with his colleagues. When he died, the *American Journal of Archaeology* printed a charming obituary by one A. M. Friend, Jr., who was presumably one of the former professors referred to in the second paragraph below. This passage is worth quoting almost in full, as much for the glimpse it affords of a gentler age in the world of archaeology as for the biographical information about the departed:

> GEORGE H. McFADDEN, a graduate of Princeton University in the class of 1930, was drowned April 19, 1953, *aet.* 46, while sailing off Cyprus. For nearly sixteen years he had been associated with, and had contributed generously to archaeological exploration on that island carried on by the University Museum, University of Pennsylvania. . . .
>
> McFadden was the inspiration and the soul of the excavations at Kourion in Cyprus. Year after year he returned home in the summer to show the results to his archaeological friends and to ask their advice and help. The last time it was a magnificent floor mosaic representing the Discovery of Achilles at Skyros, a work of the later classical period. But his interests were in all periods and phases of Greek classical civilization. His was a roving and speculative mind versed equally in literature and archaeology, and many were the evenings when he and his former professors eagerly discussed the beauty and strength of the classical spirit throughout all periods of history. McFadden had a way of making vivid and present what was so long ago to so many. This was the artist in the man. He was a fair poet and his poems ranged from a translation of Homer's Iliad into pentameters that recreated, in English, the speed and directness of the ancient poet, to excellent sonnets inspired by Thomas à Kempis' *De Imitatio Christi.* He knew his Milton by heart and loved to quote him to illustrate and enrich his own ideas.
>
> McFadden was, in fine, the reticent Classical and Christian gen-

tleman whose very profile, recalling the Emperor Augustus, was a
gauge of the beauty hidden within. It is fitting that he should find
his end in the Greek and briny sea whence came the goddess of
beauty herself to his beloved island—Cyprus.

PART THREE

A KOURION BAEDEKER

SIXTEEN HUNDRED YEARS after its violent demise, Kourion now has a booming second life as a tourist attraction. All of the guidebooks give it a star. While Cyprus possesses many beautiful antiquities, Kourion is perhaps the best restored and most attractively presented of all the archaeological sites on the island. It is situated on a lovely stretch of seacoast on the road connecting Limassol and Paphos; indeed, one can spot most of the principal attractions from the highway. Thus even those visitors who come to Cyprus for the sun and the ouzo stop for a look-see. What they find are the remains of an early Christian city, excavated from 1934 through 1954 by archaeologists affiliated with the University of Pennsylvania and then afterward by Cyprus's Department of Antiquities, under the direction of Demos Christou. We have discussed the work of George McFadden and J. F. Daniel at some length, but there were many other archaeologists attached to the American Mission, as it was called, in Kourion; the general advisor was a classicist named B. H. Hill. These archaeologists all concentrated on the sanctuary of Apollo, the Greek tombs and Bronze Age settlements nearby, and the large, latter Christian-era buildings in the city. They were aware of the ruins in the part of the city we have excavated since 1984; as we have seen, fifty years earlier J. F. Daniel had dug a trench there and discovered his "Romeo and Juliet." However, he never published this work in a scholarly way, and in any case later excavators had their hands full with other, quite interesting sites; so this part of the city site had been pretty well forgotten by the time we came along.

What follows then, is an account of the estimable Christian city that grew up on the ruins of the old pagan Kourion, when Christian cities were virtually all that were being established in the eastern Mediterranean. One may still see clearly how the city was disposed. As one enters the modern site, one first proceeds, of course, to the car park, in front of the inevitable snack bar and postcard shop. They are located next to the basilica and across the street from the forum. A northern entry to the site is under construction and the snack bar, which is situated over the ancient forum, may soon vanish ignominiously.

To begin with what must have been the spiritual focus of the new Christian Kourion, it would seem from the archaeological evidence that the basilica must have been built about fifty years after the earthquake, in the early years of the fifth century. It is a typical Early Christian episcopal building. Two rows of twelve columns created a nave flanked by two aisles; in the single apse were four columns that must have supported a baldachin, and above it no doubt was once a stately semidome.

186

Above the arches formed by the columned aisles, the sloping tiled roofs would have abutted the walls of the nave, pierced by clerestory windows, to carry the trusses of the main roof. The columns must have been quite impressive, quarried from local granite and fitted with marble bases and acanthus capitals. Almost all of this building was plundered in the Middle Ages and in the modern era as well, cannibalized for use in village architecture. Other pieces of the basilica were stolen and baked in ovens to make lime, which was used to make plaster. That strikes the modern visitor as shocking vandalism and a tragic loss, which indeed it is. Yet it is only fair: a goodly portion of the basilica had been cannibalized from classical-period buildings brought down by the earthquake.

The basilica tells us a great deal about the leaders of the Christian community that erected it, for it is at once an ambitious and a highly practical building. For the size of the congregation it must have housed, it is quite a large church. Undoubtedly the bishop of Kourion—perhaps that same Bishop Zeno who produced the manuscript of Matthew's Gospel from the grave of St. Barnabas—realized that an impressive edifice was needed for the church to thrive in the new postquake city.

The cost of building this basilica and its several subsidiary buildings—including a baptistry, a treasury, and a bishop's residence—would have been onerous to a community that must still have been reeling, at least economically, from the quake, and which had never been rich in any case. So the wise bishop improvised, using some ingenious drachma-stretching measures: wherever possible the basilica walls were superimposed over the existing foundations of the ruined Roman buildings, and much stone and marble from the old pagan city was used in the construction and decoration of its Christian successor.

This practice can result in some peculiar incongruities: on

187

the portico, one of the columns at the entryway uses for its plinth what had originally been the base of a statue of a certain Dionysios the Priest, undoubtedly a noteworthy divine from the sanctuary of Apollo. The stone must have been lifted from the abandoned sanctuary. In the corner of the inner vestibule is another statue base, this one a municipal erection, probably from the year A.D. 197, in honor of Plautus Felix Julianus, the man who was serving as the Roman governor of Cyprus at that time.

Nonetheless, there were many rich decorations commissioned especially for the basilica: the walls of the aisles and the lower part of the nave were covered with marble and panels of beautifully refined bas-relief carving. The upper parts of the nave walls were decorated with rich mosaics of colored glass, gold, and mother of pearl. The overall effect must have been quite awe-inspiring to the Kourian parishioners.

The basilica is surrounded by a cluster of subsidiary buildings. Along the north wall is a spacious paved annex, which was lined with benches and led into the narthex area at the western end. A similar annex lay along the southern side of the basilica. These two areas can almost certainly be identified as *catechumena*, places to which unbaptized converts (the catechumens, that is, those still learning their catechism) were compelled to withdraw during the celebration of the Eucharist. The comparatively great extent of these terraces suggests that a good many Kourians remained to be converted at the time the basilica was erected—and that the see was confident that it would be able to win them.

To the west of the narthex is the Diakonikon, the chapel for the presentation of gifts, its identity deduced from the presence of that quotation from Psalm 76 exhorting the faithful to "Vow, and pay to the Lord your God." It was built within the still-complete shell of a Roman building. The geometric designs of its mosaic floors served the new Christian tenants just as well as they had their pagan predecessors. A sixth-century Christian mosaic of an archangel was found on the chapel's wall, as were traces of painted plaster decoration and many sections of painted stucco moldings, both straight and arched. The latter might have fallen from a room above this money-counting sort of chapel, possibly from the bishop's residence, which, it is thought, was situated in the upper stories of these western buildings.

Adjoining this chapel is a paved open court, sloping to the west down to a hexagonal cistern, which would have been domed. In each of the six sides was a little aperture through which water could be drawn. Livestock offerings to the church were probably made here. At the bottom of the debris in the cistern was found a gold coin in excellent condition depicting Emperor Constantine IV, which was minted about 670, suggesting that soon after that time the basilica and vicinity were abandoned. The condition of the cistern leads one to suppose that the promontory location of Kourion did not have a very good water supply, which circumstance could have contributed to its abandonment.

To the southwest of the basilica is an atrium, surrounded by colonnades of four flanking porticoes. All of the column bases and shafts are cannibalized from Roman buildings brought down by the earthquakes. The rooms around the atrium are rather poorly constructed and thus suffered considerably less at the hands of scavengers.

At the bottom of a latrine, among some broken African plates, the Pennsylvanian excavators found a hoard of eighty copper coins in the tattered remains of a little sack. A. H. S. Megaw, in his essay on the basilica at Kourion, which he excavated, suggests the colorful and eminently probable hypothesis that this little treasure was hidden in the latter part of the seventh century, when the Arab raids on Cyprus began. After the basilica fell into disuse, it would appear that some squatters made their camp in the atrium. They left behind little bread ovens, along with kilns used to reduce the marble ornamentation of the church to lime. That provides a neat historical symmetry to the site: just as the Christians three hundred years before had used the earlier pagan buildings when they dominated the city, so now the Christian spiritual center served as the headquarters to its despoilers, in all likelihood Islamic raiders.

The atrium leads to the most important of the buildings dependent on the basilica: the baptistry. This structure retained its Roman mosaic floor and, like the basilica, used acanthus capitals from Roman buildings on the eight columns of the main chamber. The eastern arm of the cruciform building ends in an apse, where, on the appointed day (usually Easter), the bishop faced the assembled candidates. This apse, lined with marble and crowned with mosaic decoration, was linked with inner chambers to the east and west, all meant to accommodate the expected overflow crowd of candidates for baptism in the basilica's early days. After abjuring Satan and reciting the Nicene Creed in the presence of the bishop, the candidates processed through the inner chambers to be baptized at the font. Later, they reassembled in the main chamber in their new white robes, carrying candles, and proceeded into the basilica for their first communion.

Once all the adult Kourians had been admitted to the church, such rites perforce passed into disuse. Striking evidence of the change to infant baptism is seen in the font recess, where the steps that had led down into the water were blocked off to form a cross-shaped tank for the immersion of babies. Likewise, the capacious *catechumena* would have been used for some other purpose by this time. In its last days in the mid-seventh century, the great church must have been quite richly adorned; it was undoubtedly tempting booty to the marauding fleets of Tyre and Alexandria.

Across the way from the basilica is the Roman forum—agora in the Greek of the inhabitants—which was the heart of the city in its every incarnation. One of the most prominent features of the forum is a complicated system of cisterns dating back to the beginning of the Hellenistic period. A row of shops ran along the eastern side of this pool, making it the center of the community (which apparently always had water problems). The major remains here are of a colonnaded public building. In 1975 Cypriot archaeologists under the direction of Demos Christou found a marble fragment mentioning a "gymnasium," but Professor Christou believes that it was actually the stoa of the forum. It has been impressively restored by the Department of Antiquities with a series of limestone columns quarried locally.

In the direction of the main road, about fifteen meters west of this stoa, lie the remains of another public building, protruding from the sand blown up from the seashore. These well-hewn blocks were tumbled by the big quake of 365. Whole walls collapsed like a line of dominoes; arched doorways lie in a heap on their thresholds. Clearly, this monumental building was once quite important in the life of the city, though its exact function remains unknown. Tantalizing glimpses of its original glory can be seen in its rich decoration: an inscription to a certain high priest was found near one entrance. The walls were frescoed and the floors covered with mosaics, mainly of geometric patterns. Lozenges, guilloches, spirals, and meanders were described by cubes of black and white, yellow, green, and red.

Among the fallen ashlar blocks, the tourist will find a lovely shell-shaped niche that tumbled in the quake, which probably formed part of a fountain. A few feet to the east is a larger semicircular niche, which once had a pink marble pavement. It in turn is flanked by two more niches of similar dimensions. This site was probably a nymphaeum, a monument dedicated to the veneration of the nymphs, minor deities who were the protectresses of nature—notably water, that particularly vexatious concern of the Kourians. To the north, two column bases, two Corinthian capitals, and an elegantly spiraled, fluted column of gray marble, though all collapsed and smashed to bits, provide eloquent testimony to the former glory of this secluded place. Three kilns were constructed here in the medieval era for the purpose of reducing the statues and other marble ornamentation of the nymphaeum.

To the northwest lie the most opulent private residences yet found in Kourion, the House of the Gladiators and the House of the Achilles Mosaics. These buildings were very richly adorned, especially in mosaics, which are some of the finest in Cyprus and indeed of the whole provincial empire. Both houses were destroyed in the great earthquake.

The House of the Gladiators (so called from its mosaics depicting a gladiatorial contest, not because of any real connection with gladiators) was built around two courtyards, one small and uncolonnaded, the other larger and peristyle, which were connected by a long corridor. The area to the south of the corridor was utterly demolished; to the north lay the elaborate private bath. The latter comprised an antechamber for disrobing (the *apodyterium*), a cold bath *(frigidarium)*, a lukewarm bath *(tepidarium)*, a cruciform hot bath *(caldarium)*, a stoker's room (the *praefurnium*), and the main firing chamber *(furnus)*. The *caldarium* and *tepidarium* had the usual hypocaust system, a network of flues under the marble floors that carried the heated air.

The central open courtyard was surrounded on each side by colonnaded porticoes. The southern porch was completely lost in the earthquake, but several bases and unfluted drums belonging to the other three survive in situ and are the site of the eponymous mosaics. There were originally three panels, of which only two survive. These action pictures, commissioned by a wealthy man who was no doubt a great patron of the sports arena, are very much in the spirit of English pictures of horses and the hunt a thousand years later.

The north panel depicts two gladiators in full regalia, armed with daggers, shields, and helmets. Above their heads are their names in Greek capital letters: Hellenikos and Margareites. The central panel, which is partly damaged, shows two more armed gladiators in combat, with an unarmed man, the referee, separating them. Lytras, the gladiator at the left, is on the point of stabbing his opponent, of whose name only the initial E survives. Darios, the referee, has interposed himself in the nick of time to save E by terminating the combat. These must be portraits of real heroes of the games at the Kourion theater, less than half a mile distant. They are unique mosaics: while there was a great vogue for such realistic scenes in the late empire, nowhere else in Cyprus or indeed throughout Greece or the Middle East are there known to exist mosaic scenes of gladiatorial contests.

Mosaics are especially important to us at Kourion, because the earthquake and subsequent soil damage have utterly destroyed the paintings and other pictorial arts. Only through the durable medium of stone have the city's artistic images, and thus its civic concerns, survived. Mosaics were executed by itinerant guilds of artisans, who were commissioned by rich citizens to "paint" mythological scenes, scenes from everyday life, and geometric designs, using the medium of tiny cube-shaped stones called *tesserae,* which ranged in size from six millimeters for facial details up to two centimeters for backgrounds.

No manual for the mosaicist has survived, so one may only speculate about the techniques that were employed. We do know, however, that labor was subdivided in the workshop: the *pictor* designed the images, while the *tessellarii* actually put down the cubes in the places he indicated and laid out the geometric designs. Neutral backgrounds and simple ornamentation were pressed directly into wet plaster, called the setting bed. More complicated designs were prepared in the workshop, assembled on panels known as *emblemata,* and then inserted into the pavement.

Next to the House of the Gladiators, at the northwestern edge of the excavated city, is the House of the Achilles Mosaic, which is the first ruin one sees upon entering Kourion. In fact, it is right on the shoulder of the highway to Paphos, with the result that it is usually even dustier that the rest of the site. While the excavators are not certain about its function, Demos Christou suggests that it was a public building, constructed in the second century of the Christian era for the purpose of receiving officials or distinguished visitors. The building comprises several rooms, built on either side of a courtyard, and a colonnaded portico with mosaic floors in the usual geometric designs, which frame some unique and beautiful figurative scenes—though the scenes depicted, a hero in a dress and the abduction of a beautiful boy, might strike the modern reader as rather strange choices for a public building.

The mosaic that gives the house its name depicts the un-masking of Achilles when he was hiding among the women at the palace of Lykomedes, a post-Homeric fable narrated by Apollodorus and Ovid, among others. Thetis, Achilles' mother, knew that her son would not return from the Trojan War alive, so she disguised him as a girl and sent him to the court of Lykomedes, her friend the King of Skyros. The hero did not let it affect him too much, however, as myth tells us that while he was among the women he took Lykomedes' daughter Deidameia as his lover and fathered on her his son, Pyrrhos, later called Neoptolemos. The oracles had decreed that Achilles' participation on the Achaean side of the war against Troy was essential for victory, so Odysseus, Nestor, and Ajax were sent in search of him. Their search for the sulking, transvestite hero brought them to the palace of Lykomedes. Even so they might never have found him, except that Odysseus, nimble-witted as always, had a brainstorm. Robert Graves picks up the tale:

> Odysseus laid a pile of gifts—for the most part jewels, girdles, embroidered dresses and such—in the hall, and asked the court-ladies to take their choice. Then Odysseus ordered a sudden trum-pet-blast and clash of arms to sound outside the palace and, sure enough, one of the girls stripped herself to the waist and seized the shield and spear which he had included among the gifts. It was Achilles, who now promised to lead his Myrmidons to Troy.

Although the mosaic is not in very good condition, it vividly depicts the moment that Achilles spontaneously reveals himself to Odysseus by seizing the manly implements of war. Deidameia, his lover, is putting her left hand on his shoulder and holds his right wrist with her right hand, attempting to restrain him from leaving for the war. The blasting war trum-pet enters the scene from the right, projecting over Odysseus's head. At the left of each of the figures are their names in capital Greek letters.

Another figurative mosaic decorated the floor of a room to the southeast of the colonnaded portico. The scene here is the rape of Ganymede, which was quite a popular mythological scene. Ganymede was renowned in myth as the most beautiful boy in the world, and for that reason he was made immortal and the cupbearer to the gods. Zeus himself was enamored of the youth's beauty and desired him for his bedfellow. The father of the gods transformed himself into an eagle, swooped down to Earth, snatched up the lad from the Trojan plain, and brought him to Mount Olympos. The mosaic in the House of the Achilles Mosaic depicts the moment of the rape (in its literal sense of a seizing, rather than the later, exclusively sexual connotation), with Ganymede clasped in the talons of the eagle. Another depiction of the same scene may be found in Paphos in the House of Dionysius, which was most likely the home of Cyprus's Roman governor.

Our tour picks up with the theater, at the opposite end of the city, some five hundred yards southeast of the forum. The theater is spectacularly situated on the edge of a cliff overlooking the Mediterranean Sea. Unlike such freestanding Roman theaters as that at Salamis, the one at Kourion is carved into the north side of a gully; behind it curves away the view of the sea and the horizon. According to Christou, who excavated it, the original structure was a small Hellenistic theater dating to the second century B.C., which comprised a circular orchestra, a curved auditorium that described an arc of more than 180 degrees, and a small stage (the *skene*). Like its prototypes on the Greek mainland, the Kourion theater was a venue for productions of the classical repertory.

A theatergoer in Kourion had a view of the Mediterranean as well as of the stage. In the third century, gladiatorial fights with wild animals were presented here. The theater was completely restored in 1961 by the Cyprus Department of Antiquities. (JAMIE JAMES)

From numismatic, epigraphic, and ceramic evidence, we know that the theater was extensively remodeled during the first century after Christ, in the Roman period. This most likely took place during the reign of Nero, at the same time that the temple of Apollo was undergoing its facelift. The projecting ends of the auditorium were shortened, the orchestra was reduced to a semicircular shape, and the stage was substantially enlarged. The plays, which now included Roman dramas, were performed by well-trained actors and special dancers and singers, the chorus.

This first Roman theater was badly damaged, Christou believes, by earthquakes in A.D. 77, but at the beginning of the reign of Trajan it was remodeled and enlarged to its present size. Constructed entirely from huge limestone blocks quarried from the hillside nearby, it must have been very impressive, with a semicircular orchestra measuring seventeen meters in diameter and a rising auditorium, or *cavea*, sixty-two meters across, with seventeen rows of seats. The theater had a capacity of about 3,500 spectators. At the rear of the stage rose the straight, ornamental facade of the scene building, the *scenae frons* (literally, the forehead of the stage). This scene building rose to nearly ten meters in height and supported a great awning, perhaps of vellum, which covered most of the semicircular stage.

This grandest incarnation of the theater was decorated with spirally fluted columns and cornices. Against the east side of the theater's exterior wall three huge buttresses were added to strengthen the weak and unstable foundations. On the northeastern side of that wall a stair tower was built, which led to the upper part of the auditorium. The performances in the theater at this time must have been rather elegant. Rosewater was periodically sprinkled around the auditorium to keep it fragrant and comfortable in the noonday sun (when the performances took place, according to tradition). Archaeologist Deborah Whittingham opines that the empty rooms at the rear of the scene building held shops that sold wine and cakes to the theatergoers.

By the beginning of third century, however, drama fell from favor as the preferred form of entertainment, to be replaced by gladiatorial spectacles, including the popular hunt shows that pitted men against wild beasts, mostly imported from Africa. Inevitably, the theater was converted to this purpose. For safety reasons, the first two rows of seats were ripped out and a protective arena wall topped by a metal grill was erected around the orchestra. It was in this period that Margareites, Hellenikos, and Lytras were the prevailing champs in the arena's gladiatorial contests.

At the end of the century, tastes shifted again. Hunt spectacles were out, and drama was back in. The theater was again remodeled, for what proved to be the last time, back into a legitimate stage. It continued to be in use right up to the great quake of 365. The early Christians, never great fans of the drama, did not rebuild the theater but let it lapse into disuse. It remained in ruins for sixteen hundred years, a place to be quarried and filled with garbage, until 1961, when it was scrupulously restored by Cyprus's Department of Antiquities, which used, as had the original builders, locally quarried limestone. Now, once again, the theater is functional, offering Greek drama, Shakespeare, and musical concerts to an audience that mingles locals, tourists, and British military personnel from the neighboring air base.

In the Christian era, the bathhouse replaced the theater as the popular meeting place, and this building, as we have seen, was contributed by that devout moneybags, Eustolios. The bathing facilities he built for the city were the social center of Christian Kourion, and quite elegant they were, well equipped and lavishly ornamented with mosaics. In our account of the Church of Cyprus, in the first part of this book, we examined the mosaic inscriptions, which invoke the protection of Christ over the city, the former ward of Apollo. The baths are organized around a long, rectangular *frigidarium*, which must have been quite refreshing in the blazing summer heat. Oriented more or less north–south, the floor of the *frigidarium* is divided into four panels. The southernmost was almost entirely destroyed by the earthquake; the next section depicts a red-legged partridge, one of the many Christian symbols to be found in the baths, framed in an illusionistic ribbon motif; the third has an abstract pattern of squares and Greek keys, also called frets or meanders.

The fourth panel is one of the most intriguing mosaics in Kourion, or anywhere. Like the others, it is square, and within its frame is a large medallion depicting the head of a woman or a goddess. Inscribed around her head in Greek is the word KTICIC, or *ktisis,* which means "creation." In her right hand she holds an object resembling a builder's rule, which measures almost exactly one Roman foot in length. The female figure must be a symbolic representation of creation and thus a personification of the city's rebirth after the earthquake in its new Christian incarnation.

At the northern end of the *frigidarium* is a semicircular cold basin with a floor decorated in *opus sectile,* or inlaid marble designs; and at the eastern side was a small rectangular cold plunge bath. The latter had a sophisticated mosaic of wavelike patterns, which would have rippled cunningly when the tank was filled with water. To the west lay the *tepidarium* and the *caldarium.* The former had a marble floor over the hypocaust system, the latter a cruciform design, with the hot pools in the western and southern arms. They were oriented to the south-southwest, which enabled them to take advantage of solar heat, especially during the afternoons of cold winter months.

Hydrodynamically speaking, this was a neatly designed system. The water came from a cistern just to the north of the bathhouse, a little way up the hill, which was supplied by the Kourion aqueduct. The water was fed into the baths by gravity, the excess flowing into an ornamental pond in the house on the lower level, to the north. On its way out of the baths, the water coursed through a latrine, cleaning it as it went.

West of the baths lay the house of Eustolios, a large building of thirty-odd rooms, which exhibits characteristics both of a private residence and of a public building. Perhaps it began as the palatial villa of the wealthy Eustolios, and after his death passed into a second life as a public edifice, much the way that in the United States the mansions of rich philanthropists like J. P. Morgan and Henry Clay Frick became public institutions. The main entrance was on the western side and opened into a forecourt, which was flanked by service quarters on the left side and the latrine on the right. This court led into a vestibule, which had on its floor a mosaic inscription in black *tesserae*, surmounted by a multicolored wreath, which read: "Enter . . . and good luck to the house."

This vestibule led to a square peristyle courtyard, with a fountain and an ornamental fishpond. The porticoes facing onto this court are paved with delightful mosaics, some in an excellent state of preservation. On the northwestern and southwestern sides, the designs are complicated geometric patterns: intersecting circles, crosses, guilloches, rosettes, wave crests, and swastikas are skillfully wrought in polychrome cubes.

On the southeastern side are some of the most sophisticated Early Christian mosaics on Cyprus. Into the same sort of complex geometric designs are introduced images of birds and fish, which would have had gentle religious meaning to the Kourians of Eustolios's day. The fish, of course, would have symbolized Christ himself, and the birds were emblematic of paradise. This image is an innovation of Early Christian mosaicists—of whose work this is an early example—which became common in Greece, the Balkans, and throughout the Aegean.

The southeastern courtyard pavement is divided into four panels. The first, the best preserved, consists of four Greek crosses that meet in an eight-pointed star. In the center of the star is a delightful representation of a guinea hen, rendered in black, white, and gray marble cubes with yellow paste highlights. On each side are smaller rectangular panels in which are depicted realistic images of birds and fish. The next panel has a circle with a design of four smaller circles set on the sides of a central square. An interconnected guilloche motif surrounds each element. Rectilinear designs fill the interior spaces, with a large goose or duck set in the angles of each of the squares; especially charming is one gray goose. The other two panels are less well preserved but appear to have been purely geometric in design, with Greek crosses in the center.

It is here, in these halls, that are found the mosaic inscriptions, described in the opening chapter, that so eloquently proclaim the Christian identity of this house. In one place, this: "The sisters Reverence, Temperance, and Obedience to the law [of God] tend the platform and this fragrant hall." Elsewhere, the three lines of pseudo-Homeric dactylic hexameters, which translate, "In place of big stones and solid iron, gleaming bronze, and even adamant, this house is girt with the much-venerated signs of Christ."

Just to the east of the house of Eustolios, on the edge of the plateau, is a rectangular black and white pebble mosaic, which rests on a cobble foundation over the burial chamber of a tomb. This intriguing piece is much older than the house of Eustolios, probably dating from about 215–185 B.C., according to D. W. Rupp, the archaeologist who has studied the site. The principal surviving mosaic, edged in a wave-crest motif, is divided into two panels. The left part shows a water jar *(hydria)*, the other a dolphin and a small fish. The general layout of the floor, says

Rupp, is that of an *andron,* or men's dining hall, with space for a single *kline,* or dining couch, to be set on the southern panel. Because it is located over a chamber tomb and has a circular cutting near the threshold panel that communicates with the tomb, Rupp believes that this enigmatic mosaic may have been part of a *heroön,* a cult place for the worship of a dead person. Annual rituals of setting out a meal for the deceased in front of an empty dining couch and pouring libations into the tomb through the ceiling cutting might have taken place here.

At the foot of the cliff, just a few yards inland from the beach and thus outside Kourion proper, is the municipal cemetery, where the good burghers of the city were buried. Most of these tombs, carved into the soft limestone, were plundered in the nineteenth century by grave robbers of every persuasion. It was here, some say, that Count di Cesnola found a good part of the "Treasure of Curium." In 1940 George McFadden found ten unplundered tombs, of the late classical, Hellenistic, and Roman epochs (fourth century B.C. to the second century of the Christian era). As was often the case, the Hellenistic tombs were reused in the Roman era. The older skeletons and their grave offerings were simply shoved to the back of the space to make room for the new tenants, which makes things much easier for the archaeologist.

The Hellenistic tombs were richly furnished with burial goods, including pottery for table settings, wine decanters, vases of terracotta and alabaster that held perfume or oils, and a fine bronze jug with an acanthus leaf decoration. In one tomb McFadden found an exquisite wheel-turned bowl of colorless glass, which was inlaid with flower garlands done in colored glass. The piece was imported from Alexandria. The Roman burials held terracotta oil lamps, ceramic and glass tableware, and blown-glass jars and flasks that, when they were interred, must have contained unguents and perfumes. Also found here were wreaths of golden myrtle, gold and silver earrings set with glass and stone beads, and such practical items as bronze mirrors, tweezers, and strigils, the scrapers used by Roman athletes to wipe the sweat from their bodies. This trove is now divided up among the Kourion Museum at Episkopi, the Cyprus Museum in Nicosia, the University Museum at Penn, and the British Museum.

Andrew Oliver, an authority on ancient glass, opines in his study of the tombs that these things were presented by the living as tokens of respect to the dead, and also to seem dutiful in the eyes of their neighbors. Generally, citizens of the later Roman Empire lived with enormous pressure, approaching a cultural obsession, to appear attentive in the matter of the obsequies of their dead family members. Nonetheless, the presence of eggshells and chicken bones in context with the pottery and glass dishes indicates that these items may have served the deceased in ritual meals of the type described above.

Alongside the cemetery is a delightful chapel dedicated to and putatively containing the relics of Ayios Ermoyenis, St. Hermogenes, whose tradition at Kourion dates back to the era of the great earthquake. The tiny eighth-century Byzantine chapel, surrounded by Hellenistic and Roman cemeteries, may well be superimposed over a pagan shrine. It is beautifully situated in a grove of eucalyptus trees, next to a taverna in sight of the modern public beach.

The Greek church has three Hermogeneses, but the one who concerns us was born in Lycia (in modern Turkey) in the fourth century. He was an exceedingly holy man, who traveled throughout the Mediterranean preaching the gospel. When he became a bishop he was dispatched to Samos, where he performed numerous miracles and converted many Greeks. The governor of the island, a man named Santorinos, was an incorrigible heathen and tried everything his wicked mind could think of to make Hermogenes renounce Christ and desist in his converting ways, but the saint was steadfast in his faith. At last, mad with rage, Santorinos had Hermogenes gruesomely tortured, and he finally ordered that the worthy man be decapitated. In the dead of night, so the legend goes, some of Hermogenes' Christian brethren made off with his body and his head, placed them in a coffin, and put them out to sea. The coffin floated all the way to Kourion, where it was thrown up on the beach. The Christians here immediately built a chapel over the saint's coffin, which remains in the same place to the present day.

This tale is still told in Episkopi, and on the saint's feast day, October 5, the village celebrates with a festival in the eucalyptus grove around his chapel. Hermogenes is renowned as a healer of everything from epidemics and fever to the common cold. In order to supplicate the saint's intercession, the women of Episkopi (men are not allowed to participate) go through the village, collecting a bit of string from each household; they are all knotted together and tied around the chapel like a girdle. The string must pass over each window and the door, to bar the passage of evil spirits. This practice closely echoes the one common in ancient Greece of tying a red cord around the temple to keep out demons. Hermogenes also protects young lovers and engaged couples: a local ditty goes, "Under the olive tree of Saint Ermoyenis's chapel / I was giving you golden trinkets and you were giving me kisses."

Farther afield, halfway to the sanctuary of Apollo along the Paphos road, is the Roman stadium. It was built in the time of the Antonine emperors, in the middle part of the second century, and has the elongated U-shape characteristic of the old Greco-Roman prototypes. The word *stadium* in Latin is actually a unit of measurement equal to about 186 meters, which came to be applied to athletic edifices such as this one because they were typically one *stadium* in length. The stadium at Kourion is actually 217 meters long (and a trim 17 meters wide), but the ancients were loose and unreliable in their measurements, allowing considerable scope for local variety. It is the largest stadium known to exist in Cyprus.

It was a good three-kilometer hike from the city to the stadium, which seems strange to us moderns, but it was apparently a common practice among Greeks to site stadiums well out of town. It had seven rows of seats, which would have accommodated six thousand spectators. Only a few of the original stone seats remain, on the U-shaped bend at the western end. The use at Kourion of banked stone seating was a Roman formalization of the earlier Greek practice of seating spectators on earthen banks around the track, as at Olympia. One section of seats has been reconstructed, on the southern side.

The first stadiums were devoted to footraces, but by the time this one was built, boxing and the pentathlon (running, jumping, wrestling, tossing the javelin, and throwing the discus) were also common sports. Deborah Whittingham suggests that the stadium may have served, too, as a court for a ballgame similar to bowls, and perhaps even for team sports played with sticks or racquets. The games that were played here were most likely sponsored by the state, through the agency of the Roman governor on the island. The games usually celebrated some special imperial occasion, such as a military victory or the emperor's birthday, as well as local religious festivals, at Kourion most likely ones dedicated to Apollo, whose sanctuary is very near.

The athletes were ordinarily naked when they trained and played, though they might occasionally have worn sandals and loincloths. Perhaps it was here that St. Barnabas saw the naked heathens who provoked him to his earthquake-wreaking fury. It is possible that the stadium fell into disuse in the Christian era exactly because of such nakedness, which would have been shocking to the Christians, whose morality prohibited that sort of fleshly abandon.

Next to the stadium, on the crest of a little hill known to locals as At Meydan, which is the highest point of ground in the whole district, is a small Early Christian basilica. Constructed of beautifully finished, mostly cannibalized marble, the basilica is a fully realized example of the type favored by the Eastern church in the late fifth and early sixth centuries.

The site was first excavated in the late nineteenth century, when archaeologist H. B. Walters of the British Museum discovered, quite by accident, a bilingual dedicatory inscription in Greek and Cypro-syllabic script (the local vernacular), which reads, "Dedicated to Demeter and Kore by Hellooikos, son of Poteisis." The worship of these goddesses in tandem here is not at all strange: in the Eleusinian mysteries as practiced in Arcadia, Demeter and her daughter were venerated together, and Kourion, as we have seen, was according to tradition an Argive colony.

When Walters and his team began digging for the hoped-for classical temple to Demeter and Kore, they found instead the Early Christian basilica. Later on, however, modern excavators from the Cypriot Department of Antiquities under the direction of M. A. Christodoulou found terracotta votive figurines. They are mainly representations of female forms, which is what one would expect at an altar dedicated to two goddesses, just as the figures at Apollo's sanctuary were depictions of male forms.

The small basilica was never a principal place of worship for the Christians of Kourion, but it might have served as a locus for special festival celebrations and undoubtedly fell into desuetude in the era of the Arab raiders. It has a simple three-aisled plan. At the southern end is a spacious atrium with a large cistern in the middle of it, which, after the church was abandoned, was converted into yet another lime kiln. The atrium communicated with the narthex through three doorways in its eastern portico. The narthex in turn was linked with the nave and aisles, which were flanked by two long annexes, the *catechumena*. Just as was the case in the episcopal basilica in the city, these spaces were for the use of the unbaptized converts during the celebration of the Eucharist, which suggests that this basilica, too, dates to the earliest christianization of the district. The sanctuary of the basilica was on a slight elevation and had a large central apse flanked by two smaller ones. In the central apse may be seen the remains of the synthronon, the bench for the clergy, which would have been the bishop's throne when he was in attendance here for Mass.

The little basilica has a great deal of charm, not the least of which derives from its decidedly naïve execution. The columns, for example, are an utter hodgepodge, mixing Doric and Corinthian orders according to what was available for pilferage from the city's public buildings. Also used here were two spirally fluted columns that probably came from the theater, and some specially made limestone columns with animal capitals. And in 1974 Cypriot archaeologists discovered that some of the marble plaques used in the flooring were actually classical bas-relief panels, their pagan images simply turned over face down. One of them depicts the story of Amymone and Poseidon.

Amymone was one of the fifty daughters of Danaos and Europe, of whom all but one murdered their husbands on their wedding nights. When she lay with Poseidon in drought-stricken Argos, the Spring of Lerna gushed forth from the ground, which is the scene depicted in the panel at the small basilica. The other is a sensitively incised head of a water nymph. These plaques, dated to between A.D. 250 and 450, were probably taken from a late Roman building. Because they are depictions of water nymphs, Vassos Karageorghis has speculated that they might have come from the nymphaeum that housed the city's water supply.

AFTERWORD

AN EXCAVATION such as the one at Kourion—like any major archaeological undertaking—is never finished. This is true in the most basic sense, for just a quick glance around the site shows me another ten or twenty years of work. In fact, the city of Kourion could well keep excavators busy for another hundred years, if they do it right. I sometimes threaten my students that I may have my body frozen as Walt Disney did, have myself thawed out after they have finished, and come back to make sure they did it right.

Yet even after the last rock and spadeful of dirt from a dig have been carted away and after one has studied every scrap, down to the final insignificant olive pit and rusty nail, the place lives on in your head, which is where it was all along. An excavation like ours, which seeks to reconstruct the quality and flavor of ancient life, does so not in the bits and pieces one finds but rather in the armature, entirely intellectual, that one builds to hold the pieces together.

It is exciting; we hope that this account has conveyed that much, at least. Yet it can be terribly frustrating. One becomes involved with an excavation in much the way that one is involved with life: perhaps that is because, more than any other discipline, archaeology is a microcosm of life, embracing as it does the whole range of human activity. Yet precisely because of that fact, an excavation at times will be, for the people who are carrying it out, infuriatingly incomplete, full of small random gaps. No matter how complete the picture one draws may become—and in the case of Kourion, we have filled it in tolerably well—there is always another connection to be made, some feature that is still a bit fuzzy. One's understanding of the place is always provisional. In some cases this may be literally true: an identification of a pot, for example, or a classicist's interpretation of a passage in a work of literature, can only be based upon the best scholarship available at the moment. And that changes. What is indisputably true one season becomes the outmoded fallacy of the next.

We archaeologists are all connected to one another by a giant, rather ungainly web, which consists of articles in scholarly journals, mimeographed newsletters, and slide lectures at the ceaseless round of conventions, all of which seem to be held in the same place, the Marriot–Hilton platonic form of hotel. There we keep shaking up one another's ideas. It can be deadly dull, of course, but it can also be exciting: I know beyond doubt that someday, perhaps next year, perhaps thirty years from now when I am a doddering emeritus professor, I will read an article in an obscure journal, or hear a lecture by some struggling assistant professor, that will change, perhaps radically, my thinking about Kourion. Far from daunting one, it is just that that keeps one going.

For the rewards are large and deep, and as time goes on at a dig, they get to be more and more so. The intimacy that exists between an archaeologist and the people he is excavating can be quite startling in its profundity. It is true that Camelia, the middle-aged laboring man, the young Christian family had all been dead for more than sixteen hundred years when we unearthed them; it is just that distance that forged the deep connection between us. There is nothing more personal than death. Camelia left this world all alone (except for the company of her mule), and she remained utterly alone until we butted in. She did not invite us, but she has graciously attended us and answered every question we have put to her; and over the course of the excavation, something very like friendship has flourished between us.

That is no mere sentimentalism: Cicero said that a friend is a second self, and it is in that light that we at the Kourion dig have come to regard the people whose lives we have so presumptuously entered. A study like this one only has meaning if one relates to it on the most basic and human level. The folks who lived in Kourion dreamed and napped and told lies and burned up with love and occasionally ate and drank too much, just like some people we know, just like us. The deeper into the rubble you dig, the more vividly you feel it: "It could have been me out there, talking to a hysterical mule. It could have been my wife and child, screaming with terror." That is what makes it at once so rewarding and, as I say, so frustrating. For, as in any friendship, not all of the gaps ever get filled in.

Your best friend has secrets he is never going to share with you; and so for an excavator there is always a quality of mystery, a final shadowy little corner that will never be revealed.

That's what keeps us digging.

BIBLIOGRAPHY

Ambraseys, N. N. *The Seismic History of Cyprus*. 1965.

Ammianus Marcellinus. John C. Rolfe, trans. Cambridge, Mass., 1935–39.

Baring-Gould, Sabine. *The Lives of the Saints*. London, 1872–1877.

Barker, Philip. *Techniques of Archaeological Excavation*. 1977.

Benson, J. L. *Bamboula at Kition*. Philadelphia, 1972.

Bikai, Patricia M. *The Pottery of Tyre*. Warminster, 1978.

Boethius, Axel, and Ward-Perkins, J. B. *Etruscan and Roman Architecture*. Baltimore, 1970.

Carnandet, Johann, ed. *Acta Sanctorum*. Paris, 1863–1920.

Cesnola, L. P. di. *Cyprus: Its Ancient Cities, Tombs, and Temples*. London, 1877.

Christou, Demos. *Kourion: A Complete Guide to Its Monuments and Local Museum*. Nicosia, Cyprus, 1986.

Chronicon Paschale. J.-P. Migne, ed. *Patrologia Graeca*, vol. 92.

Cox, Dorothy H. *Coins from the Excavations at Curium 1932–1953.* New York, 1959.

Deneauve, Jean. *Lampes de Carthage.* Paris, 1969.

Gjerstad, E. *Greek Geometric and Archaic Pottery Found in Cyprus.* Stockholm, 1977.

————. *The Swedish Cyprus Expedition.* Stockholm, 1937.

Gunnis, Rupert. *Historic Cyprus.* Reprinted, Nicosia, Cyprus, 1973.

Hayes, J. W. *Late Roman Pottery.* London, 1972.

————. *A Supplement to Late Roman Pottery.* London, 1980.

Herodotus. *The Histories.* Aubrey de Sélincourt, trans. London, 1954.

Hill, Sir George. *A History of Cyprus.* Cambridge, 1949.

Hodge, T. *The Woodwork of Greek Roofs.* Cambridge, 1960.

Jerome. *Chronicon.* J.-P. Migne, ed. *Patrologia Latine,* vol. 27.

————. *Commentarium in Isaiam Prophetam.* J.-P. Migne, ed. *Patrologia Latine,* vol. 24.

————. *Vita S. Hilarionis.* J.-P. Migne, ed. *Patrologia Latine,* vol. 23.

Karageorghis, Vassos. *The Ancient Civilizations of Cyprus.* Geneva, 1969.

————. *Cyprus: From the Stone Age to the Romans.* London, 1982.

————. *Salamis.* New York, 1969.

Lane Fox, Robin. *Pagans and Christians.* New York, 1986.

McFadden, George H. "Cyprus." *American Journal of Archaeology* 55 (1951).

————. "Cyprus 1950–1951." *American Journal of Archaeology* 56 (1952).

————. "The Sanctuary of Apollo." *University of Pennsylvania Bulletin* 7:2 (1938).

————. "Sanctuary of Apollo at Kourion." *University of Pennsylvania Bulletin* 8:4 (1940).

Mitford, Terence. *The Inscriptions of Kourion.* Philadelphia, 1971.

Murray, A. S. *Excavation in Cyprus.* London, 1900.

Myres, J. L. *Handbook of the Cesnola Collection of Antiquities from Cyprus.* New York, 1914.

Orosius, Paulus. *Historiae.* J.-P. Migne, ed. *Patrologia Latine,* vol. 31.

Purcell, H. D. *Cyprus.* New York, 1968.

Robertson, Ian. *Blue Guide to Cyprus.* London, 1981.

Socrates Scholasticus. *Historia Ecclesiastica.* J.-P. Migne, ed. *Patrologia Graeca,* vol. 67.

Sozomenus. *Historia Ecclesiastica.* J.-P. Migne, ed. *Patrologia Graeca,* vol. 67.

Spyridakis, Constantinos. *A Brief History of Cyprus.* Nicosia, Cyprus, 1974.

Swiny, H. W., ed. *An Archaeological Guide to the Ancient Kourion Area and the Akrotiri Peninsula.* Nicosia, Cyprus, 1982.

Taylor, J. du Plat, and Megaw, A. H. S. *Cyprus.* 1968.

Tomkins, Calvin. *Merchants and Masterpieces.* New York, 1970.

Young, John, and Young, Suzanne. *Terracotta Figures from Kourion in Cyprus.* Philadelphia, 1955.

INDEX

ABOUT THE AUTHORS

DAVID SOREN is a pioneer in seismic archaeology, the excavation of cities buried by earthquakes. His identification of the Kourion earthquake with the one in the ancient historian Ammianus Marcellinus's vivid eyewitness account made his reputation in 1980.

Soren not only is an archaeologist, but has degrees in art history and ancient literature as well. He graduated Phi Beta Kappa from Dartmouth and received his Ph.D. in classics at Harvard. By the age of thirty-two he was the chairman of the Department of Art History and Archaeology at the University of Missouri. He is now head of the classics department at the University of Arizona, where he also teaches classes in art history and cinema. His seven-year appointment as guest curator and lecturer at the American Museum of Natural History in New York City began in 1979.

JAMIE JAMES was born and raised in Houston, Texas, and graduated from Williams College. Upon graduation he wrote a sports column for *Andy Warhol's Interview*. Since that time he has been a frequent contributor to *Rolling Stone, Life, Discover, Sports Illustrated, The Nation*, and *Connoisseur*, as well as the New York *Times*, the Los Angeles *Times*, and *The Guardian*. He lives in New York City.